BEGINNER'S GUIDE

TO

WINDOWS 10

Learning the essentials

SIMEON E

COPYRIGHT

All rights researched. No part of this publication, Beginner's guide to windows 10, may be reproduced or used in any manner without the written permission of the copyright owner except for the use of quotations in a book review.

Printed in the United States of America
© 2021 by Simeon Edward

Table of Contents

COPYRIGHT ii
INTRODUCTION 1
SECTION ONE - GETTING STARTED 1
    1.1. IDENTIFYING YOUR WINDOWS 10 EDITION 1
    1.2 GETTING WINDOWS 10 FROM MICROSOFT STORE 2
    1.3. UNLOCKING YOUR DESKTOP SCREEN 3
SECTION TWO - INTERACTING WITH YOUR DESKTOP 4
    2.1 DESKTOP AREA 4
    2.2 START BUTTON/ WINDOWS LOGO KEY 4
    2.3 WINDOWS 10 START MENU...5
        2.3.1 LOCKING YOUR SCREEN FROM THE START MENU 6
        2.3.2 CHANGING THE START MENU DISPLAY TO WINDOWS 8..6
        2.3.3 CUSTOMIZING FOLDERS ON START..................................7
        2.3.4 CHANGING THE BACKGROUND COLOR OF YOUR START MENU. 8
        2.3.5 MANAGING AND ORGANIZING START TILES.....................9
    2.4 WINDOWS TASKBAR 11
        2.4.1 PINNING YOUR APPLICATIONS TO THE TASKBAR 12
        2.4.2 LOCKING AND UNLOCKING THE TASKBAR 13
        2.4.3 ACCESSING THE WINDOWS TASK MANAGER..................15
    2.5 WINDOWS ACTION CENTER...16
        2.5.1 COLLAPSING THE TILES IN THE ACTION CENTRE 17
SECTION THREE - SETTING UP YOUR WINDOWS 10 18
    3.1 CREATING A MICROSOFT ACCOUNT 18

3.2	FAMILY ACCOUNTS AND PARENTAL CONTROL	20
3.3	SIGN-IN OPTIONS	23
3.4	PERSONALIZING YOUR LOCK SCREEN	24
3.4.1	CORTANA LOCK SCREEN SETTINGS	27
3.5	CUSTOMIZING THE BACKGROUND SETTINGS	28
3.5.1	PICTURE	28
3.5.2	SLIDESHOW	29
3.5.3	SOLID COLOR	31
3.6	CHOOSING THE RIGHT THEMES FOR YOUR WINDOWS 10	32
SECTION FOUR - USING THE WINDOWS 10 SETTINGS		34
4.1	DATE AND TIME SETTINGS	34
4.2	ADDITIONAL CLOCK AND REGION SETTINGS	35
4.3	SYSTEM SETTINGS	36
4.3.1	DISPLAY SETTINGS	36
4.3.2	CUSTOMIZING THE SOUND SETTINGS	37
4.3.3	NOTIFICATIONS SETTINGS	39
4.3.4	USING THE FOCUS ASSIST	42
4.3.5	NEARBY SHARING	43
4.3.6	POWERING OPTIONS FOR YOUR DEVICE	44
4.3.7	CUSTOMIZING YOUR BATTERY SETTINGS	50
4.4	EASE OF ACCESS SETTINGS	52
4.4.1	DISPLAY SETTINGS	54
4.4.2	CURSOR AND POINTER	55
4.4.3	COLOR FILTERS	57
4.4.4	HIGH CONTRAST	58

		4.4.5	USING WINDOWS NARRATOR 59

- 4.4.5 USING WINDOWS NARRATOR 59
- 4.4.6 SPEECH: Talk instead of type 61
- 4.4.7 KEYBOARD 63
- 4.4.8 MOUSE 64
- 4.5 WORKING WITH TABLET MODE 65
- 4.5.1 SWITCHING TO TABLET MODE 65
- 4.5.2 CUSTOMIZING THE TABLET MODE 65
- 4.5.3 SWITCHING FROM TABLET MODE TO DESKTOP MODE .. 67

SECTION FIVE - WINDOWS 10 APPLICATIONS 68

- 5.1 MICROSOFT STORE 68
- 5.2 USING THE CORTANA APP 69
- 5.2.1 PERSONALIZING YOUR CORTANA SETTINGS 70
- 5.2.2 SETTING THE ALARM WITH CORTANA. 71
- 5.2.3 SEARCHING FOR INFORMATION ON YOUR COMPUTER .72
- 5.2.4 SEARCHING INFORMATION ON THE WEB WITH CORTANA 73
- 5.2.5 PERFORMING CALCULATIONS WITH CORTANA 74
- 5.2.6 SHUTTING DOWN YOUR LAPTOP WITH CORTANA 74
- 5.3 USING MICROSOFT EDGE BROWSER 75
- 5.3.1 FEATURES OF MICROSOFT EDGE BROWSER 76
- 5.4 USING THE WINDOWS 10 CALCULATOR 81
- 5.4.1 DATE CALCULATION 84
- 5.4.2 CONVERTER 84
- 5.5 USING THE VIDEO EDITOR 87
- 5.6 CHANGING WINDOWS DEFAULT APPS 88
- 5.7 UNINSTALLING APPLICATIONS 90

	5.7.1	SHORTCUT METHOD 90
	5.7.2	UNINSTALLING FROM THE CONTROL PANEL 90

SECTION SIX - WINDOWS FILE EXPLORER 92

	6.1	HOME TAB 93
	6.2	SHARE TAB 94
	6.3	VIEW TAB. 95

SECTION SEVEN - MANAGING DEVICE CONNECTIONS 98

	7.1	BLUETOOTH CONNECTIONS 98
	7.2	CONNECTING TO A PEN DRIVE 100
	7.3	WI-FI CONNECTIONS 100
	7.4	USING THE MIRACAST 102
	7.5	CONNECTING TO PRINTER 103

SECTION EIGHT - WINDOWS 10 SECURITY 105

	8.1	VIRUS AND THREAT PROTECTION 105
	8.1.1	CURRENT THREATS 106
	8.1.2	VIRUS & THREAT PROTECTION SETTINGS 108
	8.2	ACCOUNT PROTECTION 109
	8.3	FIREWALL & NETWORK PROTECTION 109
	8.3.1	ALLOWING AN APPLICATION THROUGH THE FIREWALL 110
	8.3.2	NETWORK AND INTERNET TROUBLESHOOTER 111
	8.3.3	FIREWALL NOTIFICATION SETTINGS 111
	8.3.4	ADVANCED SETTINGS 111
	8.3.5	RESTORE FIREWALLS TO DEFAULT 112
	8.4	APPS & BROWSER CONTROL 112
	8.5	DEVICE SECURITY 113

  8.5.1 SECURITY PROCESSOR 113

  8.5.2 SECURE BOOT 114

 8.6 DEVICE PERFORMANCE & HEALTH 114

SECTION NINE – ADDITIONAL WINDOWS 10 FEATURES 115

 9.1 TIPS AND TRICKS IN WINDOWS 10 115

  9.1.1 USING EMOJIS 115

  9.1.2 USING THE SNIP AND SKETCH TOOL 115

  9.1.3 WINDOWS SNAPPING 116

  9.1.4 CUSTOMIZING YOUR WINDOWS UPDATE 119

  9.1.5 USING THE XBOX GAME BAR FOR SCREEN CAPTURE 120

  9.1.6 RUNNING THE TROUBLESHOOTER 122

  9.1.7 USING THE MAGNIFIER 123

  9.1.8 USING STEPS RECORDER 125

  9.1.9 CUSTOMIZING YOUR STARTUP APPS 125

  9.1.10 SHAKE TOOL: 127

  9.1.11 WORKING WITH MULTIPLE DESKTOPS: 127

  9.1.12 ACCESSING APPLICATIONS ON THE TASKBAR 128

  9.1.13 USING WINDOWS 10 VOICE RECORDER 128

  9.1.14 QUICK ASSIST 130

  9.1.15 TROUBLESHOOTING OPTIONS FOR WINDOWS 10 131

 9.2 WINDOWS 10 SHORTCUTS 134

INTRODUCTION

Windows 10 is one of the fastest and most stable operating systems developed and coordinated by Microsoft. It was released to the general public on the 29th of July 2015 with enormous benefits over the previous versions. Windows 10 can work on many devices such as Smartphones, Tablets, and Laptops.

Compared with previous Windows versions, such as Windows 7 and Windows 8.1, Windows 10 is provided with many added features such as Cortana, Xbox game bar, and Microsoft Edge browser. These features have led to enhanced performance, improved security, and a good user experience.

This user's guide will introduce you to key features and tools within Windows 10 operating system. You will also learn some tips and tricks alongside few Windows 10 troubleshooting techniques.

SECTION ONE - GETTING STARTED

Once you have windows 10 installed on your device, I believe it should be easy to get you started.

1.1. IDENTIFYING YOUR WINDOWS 10 EDITION

There are five different editions of the Windows 10 Operating System:

- **<u>Windows 10 Home</u>:** For most users, this edition is sufficient to execute their tasks. Windows 10 home consists of most key features such as Cortana, Miracast, Microsoft Edge, and Tablet mode.
- **<u>Windows 10 Pro</u>:** This is a more advanced and costlier edition of Windows 10 compared to Windows 10 home. It is usually needed and utilized by businesses and some experts in information technology who require added features within their operating systems. Some of the features in Windows 10 Pro are; Hyper-V virtualization, Remote access services, and BitLocker Drive Encryption.
- **<u>Windows 10 Enterprise and Education:</u>** This edition has more advanced security functions, and is utilized by large schools and businesses. In addition to Windows 10 Pro features, Windows 10 Enterprise and Education has other tools such as a Long-term servicing branch and device guard.

Other editions are the **Windows 10 mobile** and **Windows 10 Internet of things**
To identify your Windows 10 edition;
Press Windows logo key + Pause on your keyboard
or Windows logo key + fn + Pause for some users.

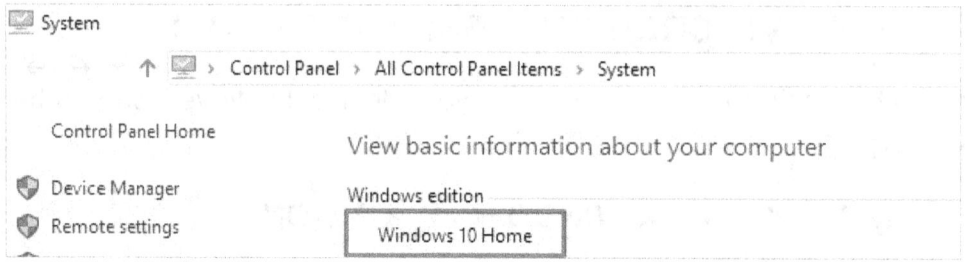

1.2 GETTING WINDOWS 10 FROM MICROSOFT STORE

The operating system upgrade is free for licensed Windows 7 and 8 users. However, you can get a new Windows 10 from Microsoft Store and install it on your device.

To install Windows 10 from the store;
1. Go to www.microsoft.com/store
2. Type Windows 10 home or Windows 10 pro on the search bar
3. You can download using the **'download'** or the **'USB'** icon.

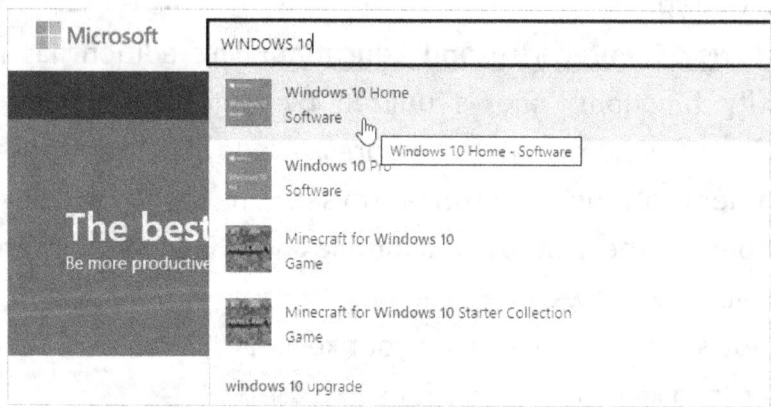

It is important to know the system requirement and ensure that your system is compatible with the version to be downloaded.

1.3. UNLOCKING YOUR DESKTOP SCREEN

Switching on your device is quite easy. All you need to do is locate and press the power button. When you power on your computer for the first time, you will have to follow the instructions provided on the screen to personalize your device. However, if you have already created a username and password, you should;

1. Click anywhere on the lock screen
2. Select your account
3. Type your password
4. Press Enter.

SECTION TWO - INTERACTING WITH YOUR DESKTOP

After signing in to your device, you will be able to access the desktop screen. From the desktop environment, you can navigate anywhere, and conveniently manage your applications.

The Windows desktop environment consists of;
- The Main desktop area.
- Start Button
- Windows Taskbar
- Action center

2.1 DESKTOP AREA

Everyone wants an easy way of getting their information whenever it is needed. One of the ways to do this is by saving such data in the desktop area. The area may consist of files or folders and applications icons such as recycle bin.

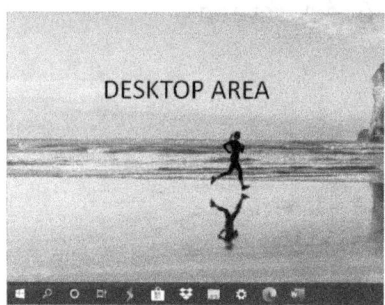

2.2 START BUTTON/ WINDOWS LOGO KEY

The windows start button is one of the most important and powerful features in windows 10. With a click of the button, you can gain access to any information on your PC. Also, pressing the Windows logo key with some other keys gives you quick access to pages and information that would have taken more time to access. For example, pressing the **Windows key + D** takes you back to your desktop screen.

2.3 WINDOWS 10 START MENU

The windows start menu allows you to quickly access your information such as profile, files, and saved applications.

The start menu in Windows 10 is slightly different from what we had in windows 7 and 8. A section of the start menu that resembles Windows 7 is known as the app list. On the other hand, the start tiles on the right side resembles windows 8 start menu. Therefore, Windows 10 is a hybrid of Windows 7 and Windows 8 start menu.

To access your start menu, do the following;
Click on the start button in the desktop environment, just beside the search box or Press the Windows logo key on your keyboard.

The Start menu consists of;
- Start: By default, the start may consist of files such as the document, user account, pictures, system settings, and Power option.
- Recently added files or application list
- Start tiles: This start tiles consist of Live tiles, applications, folders and other user information.

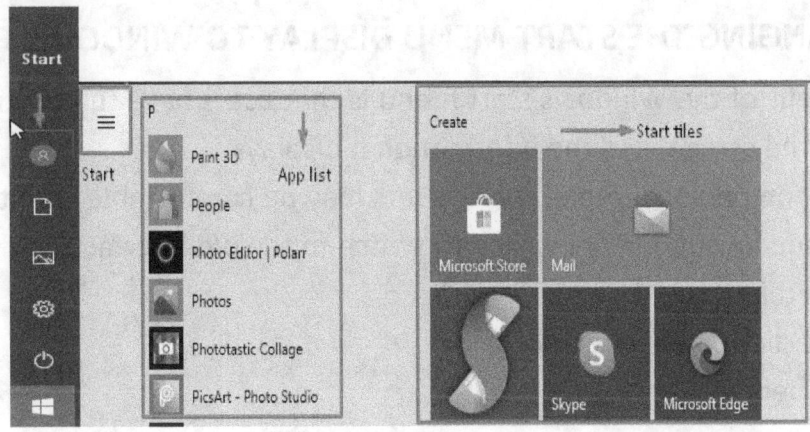

2.3.1 LOCKING YOUR SCREEN FROM THE START MENU

Let us think of a situation when you are compiling your weekly report and you suddenly receive a call for an impromptu meeting with your company's managing director. Since you have an unfinished task, it may become necessary to lock your device for a short period.

To lock your computer screen;
1. Press the Windows logo key on your keyboard to access the start menu.
2. Click on the user account icon and select lock.

Alternatively;
1. Click Ctrl + Alt + Delete
2. Click the Lock option

2.3.2 CHANGING THE START MENU DISPLAY TO WINDOWS 8

A key benefit of the Windows start menu is that users have full control of how it appears on the screen, and the information it displays.

Depending on personal preferences, users may be comfortable with the windows 8.1 start menu layout and are willing to switch to the old interface.

To achieve this;
1. Right-click on your desktop area
2. Click personalize.

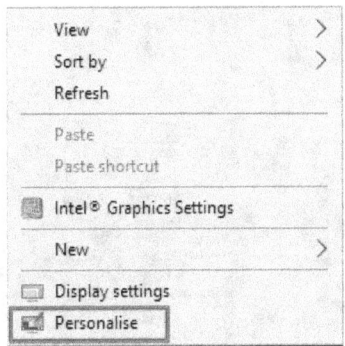

3. Click on **Start**

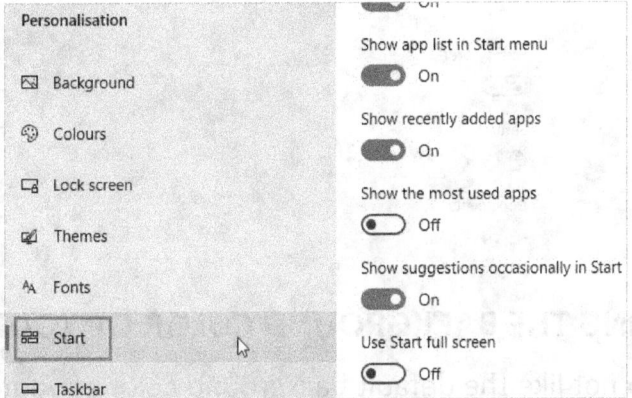

4. Toggle on '**Use start full screen**'.
5. Confirm the new start menu layout by pressing the Windows logo key on your keyboard.

2.3.3 CUSTOMIZING FOLDERS ON START

To select which of your applications show on the start section of Windows 10 start menu;

1. Right-click on the desktop area and click on **Personalize**
2. Select **Start**
3. Click the '**choose which folders appear on the start link.**

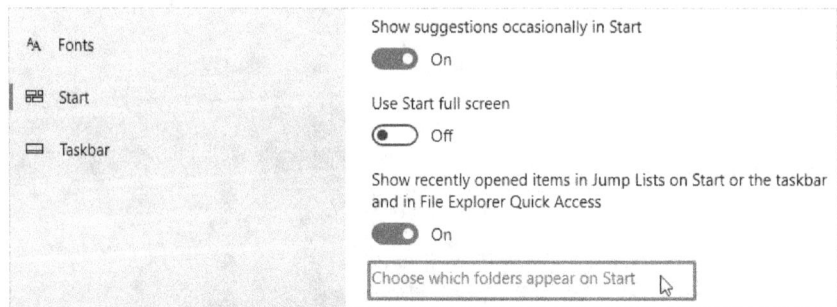

4. Toggle on or off the applications based on your preference.

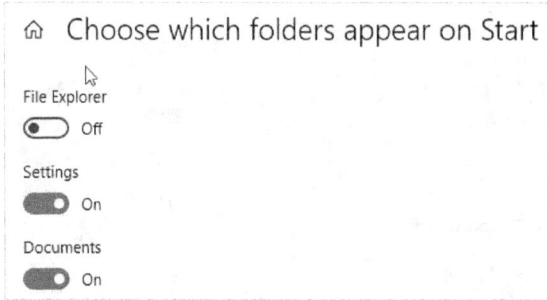

2.3.4 CHANGING THE BACKGROUND COLOR OF YOUR START MENU.

What if you do not like the default background color of your start menu, and you feel like changing it to suit your taste? You need to;
1. Right-click on your desktop area and click personalize.
2. Select **Colors**
3. Select your preferred color from the **'choose your color'** menu.

If you select light or dark, your choice will reflect immediately. However, if you select the customize option from the menu, you will choose your default windows and app mode.

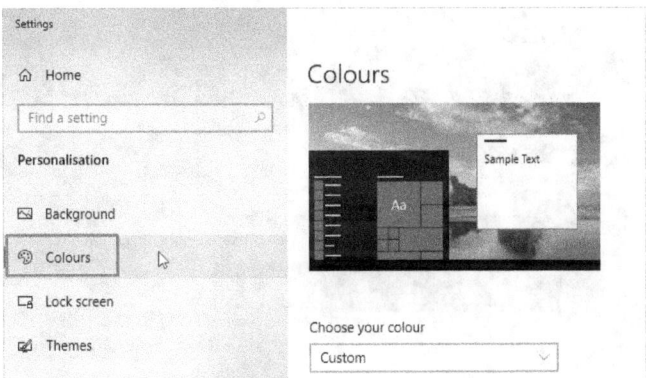

4. Switch on or off the **transparency effects** toggle
5. Select your preferred accent color from the available options or check the '**Automatically pick an accent color from my background**' check box.

2.3.5 MANAGING AND ORGANIZING START TILES

There is nothing like the benefits and the feel-good effects that you get when your applications are well organized in the windows start menu. There are options available for users to personalize and logically arrange applications in the start menu.

> ➤ **RESIZING YOUR START TILES**

To resize the start tiles;
1. Press the Windows logo key on your keyboard to access your start menu
2. Right-click on the tile you wish to resize
3. Place the mouse on the resize option and choose your preferred size.

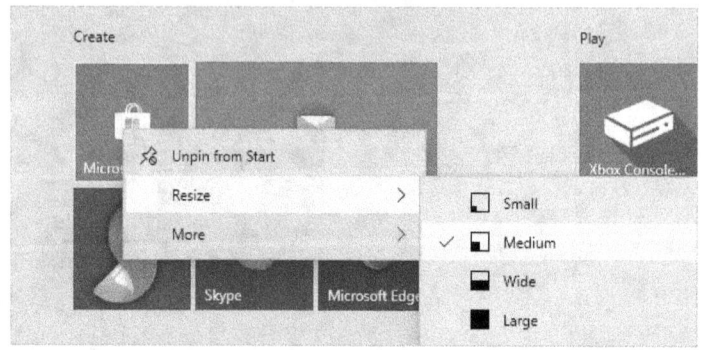

> **ARRANGING START TILES IN FOLDERS**

You can organize your application tiles in a folder within the start menu. Doing this will make it easy for you to access and work on different applications. For instance, you can classify Microsoft office applications such as MS Word, Excel, and MS PowerPoint together in a folder while organizing your browsers in another folder.

To organize your applications in a folder;
1. Press the Windows logo key or click on the start button to access the start menu
2. From the start menu, search for your preferred application in the app list by scrolling down the list.
3. Drag the application from the list towards an existing application on the start tiles to create a new folder. However, you can drag and drop the application into an existing folder if it has already been created.

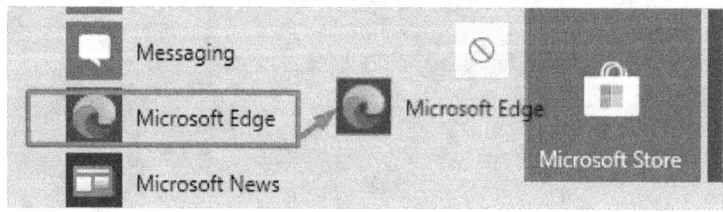

4. To name your folder, click directly on the folder and type the name in the **Name folder** box.

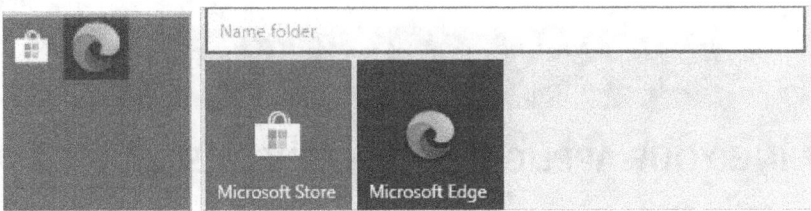

You can also categorize your tiles into a group. To achieve this;
1. Drag and drop the tile into any group of your choice
2. Click the equality symbol above the group to name it.

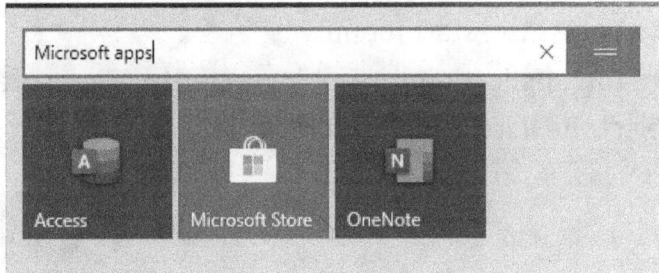

2.4 WINDOWS TASKBAR

The windows taskbar is another helpful feature in Windows. It allows you to pin your frequently used applications, files, and browser on your desktop. Pinning your applications reduces the time to search for information and increases the overall efficiency. The Windows 10 taskbar may consist of the search box, file explorer, task view, and more based on the user's preference.

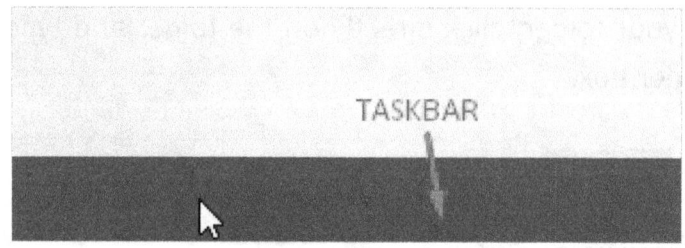

2.4.1 PINNING YOUR APPLICATIONS TO THE TASKBAR

We all have our frequently used applications, and our work becomes much faster if we access them quickly. One of the ways to do this is by pinning those applications to the taskbar.

For example, to pin Microsoft office word to the Windows taskbar;
1. Click on the Windows start button or press the Windows logo key on your keyboard to access the start menu.
2. Scroll down the application list until you get to Microsoft Office Word. You can also select the # icon and then click W to access Microsoft office word.

3. Right-click on the MS Word application and place your pointer on **More**
4. Select **Pin to taskbar.**

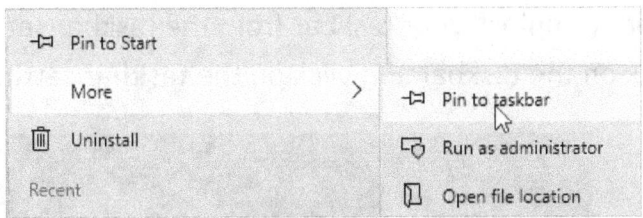

Alternatively;
1. Type **Word** in the search box to display the application
2. Right-click on the word and click on **Pin to taskbar**.

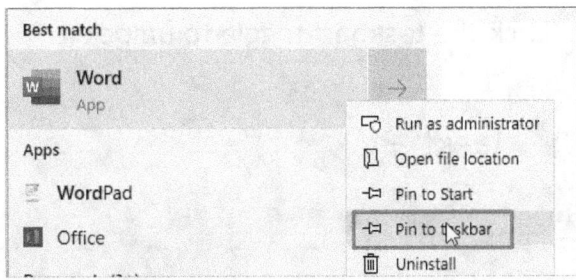

2.4.2 LOCKING AND UNLOCKING THE TASKBAR

Your taskbar is likely locked in position by default. However, you can unlock the taskbar if you chose to pin more applications. To unlock your taskbar;
1. Place your pointer on the taskbar
2. Right-click on the taskbar
3. Click on the '**Lock the task'** bar option.

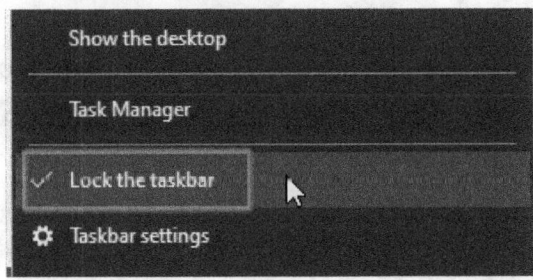

You can also lock or unlock your taskbar from the taskbar settings. To do this;
1. Right-click on the taskbar and click on the **taskbar settings**.

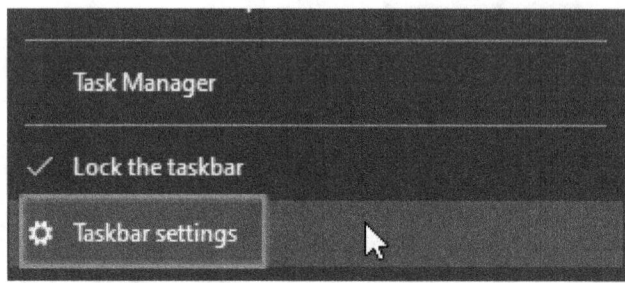

2. Switch off the **'Lock the taskbar'** toggle to unlock it.

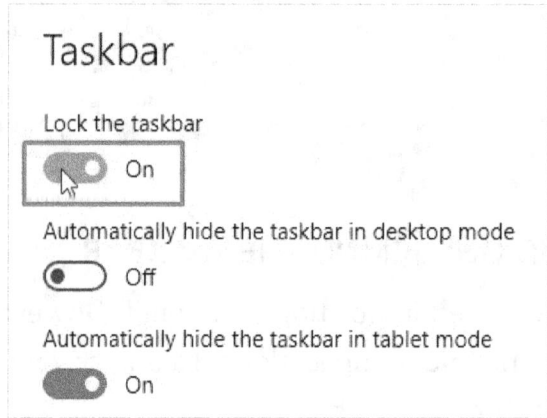

You can hide the taskbar from your desktop by switching on the '**Automatically hide the taskbar in the desktop mode**' toggle. You can switch other toggles in the taskbar settings based on your preferences.

It is possible to change the location of your taskbar from the bottom of the desktop screen to the top, right or left. The personalization is done in the taskbar settings.
1. From the taskbar settings, scroll down to the **Taskbar location on the screen**.

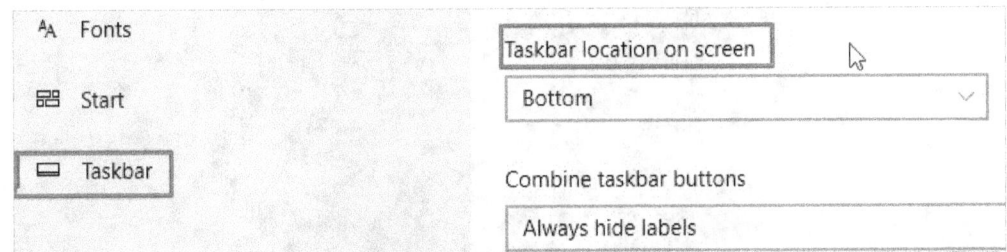

2. Select 'Right,' 'Left,' or 'Top' from the drop-down menu to position the windows taskbar at the right, left, or the top of your Windows 10 desktop, respectively.

There is an option available on settings to label the applications pinned on the taskbar. To customize this setting, scroll down to the '**combine taskbar buttons**' and select the preferred option from the drop-down menu.

- To return to your desktop, press Windows key + D

2.4.3 ACCESSING THE WINDOWS TASK MANAGER

The task manager helps you keep track of all the applications and files running on your computer, including startup apps. You can optimize or speed up your device using the task manager by disabling applications or files affecting your system's performance.

To access the Task Manager;
1. Right-click on the taskbar
2. Click on **Task manager**

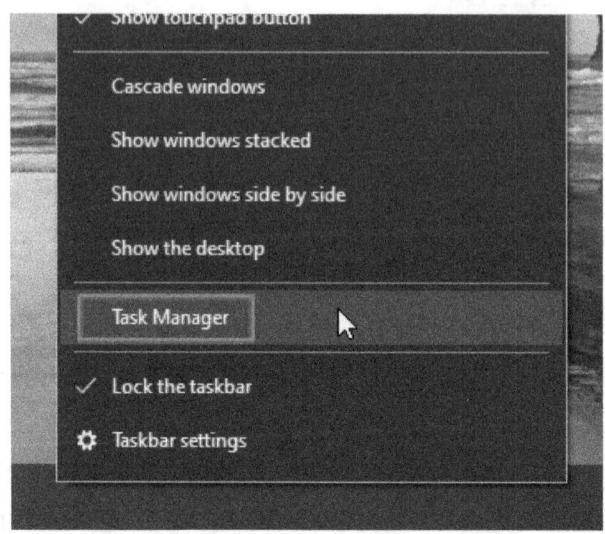

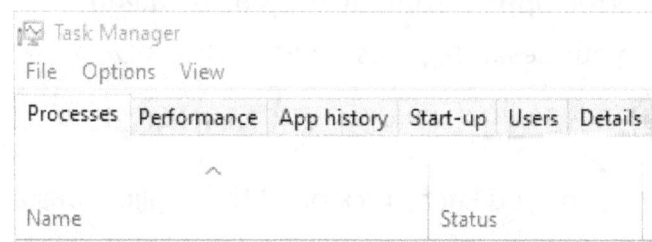

To stop the applications or background processes affecting the system's performance, select the application and click on **End Task** at the bottom section of the task manager.

2.5 WINDOWS ACTION CENTER

The windows action center helps you to manage some of the applications on your device easily.

Windows action center is the speech bubble icon located on the right side of the taskbar.

The upper part of the action center is the notification area where you receive notifications such as important system updates. The lower part contains some essential application tiles or quick access.

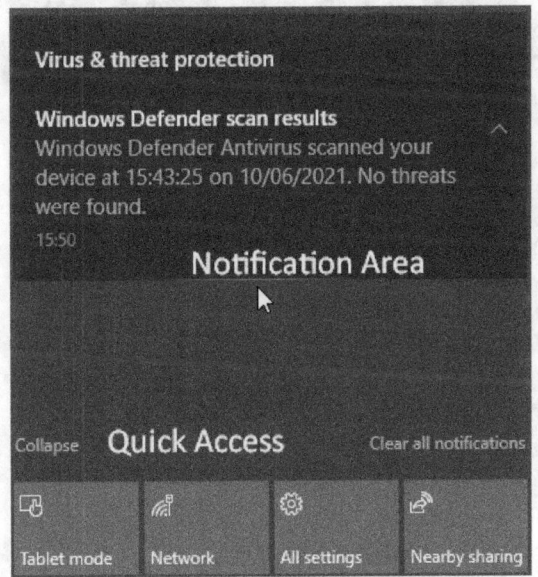

2.5.1 COLLAPSING THE TILES IN THE ACTION CENTRE

As a user, you may want to reduce the number of tiles that show on your quick access or action center environment. To achieve this;

1. Click on the action center icon or press Windows key + A to open the action center.
2. Click on **Collapse** to minimize the tiles, or click on **Expand** to expand the tiles.

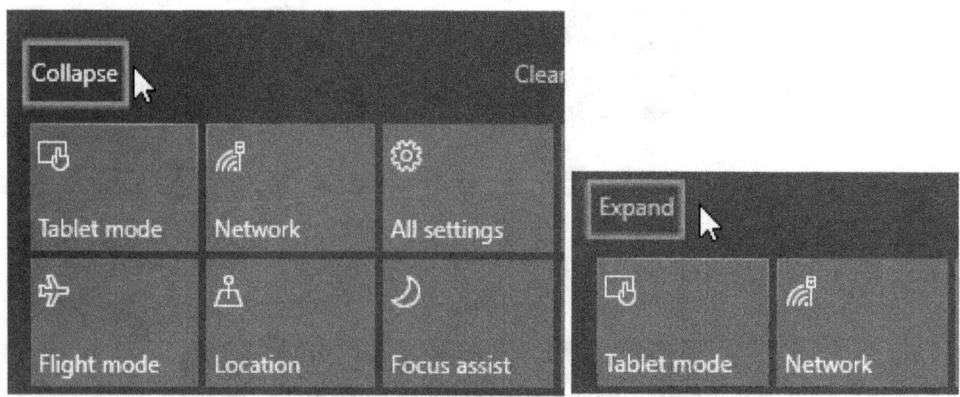

SECTION THREE - SETTING UP YOUR WINDOWS 10

3.1   CREATING A MICROSOFT ACCOUNT

Creating a Microsoft account gives you access to a wide variety of services offered by Microsoft. Some of the benefits include but not limited to the storage of information on One drive, making use of Microsoft outlook for communication, and making the best use of Microsoft services.

To create a Microsoft account;
1. 1. Go to start > Settings > Accounts

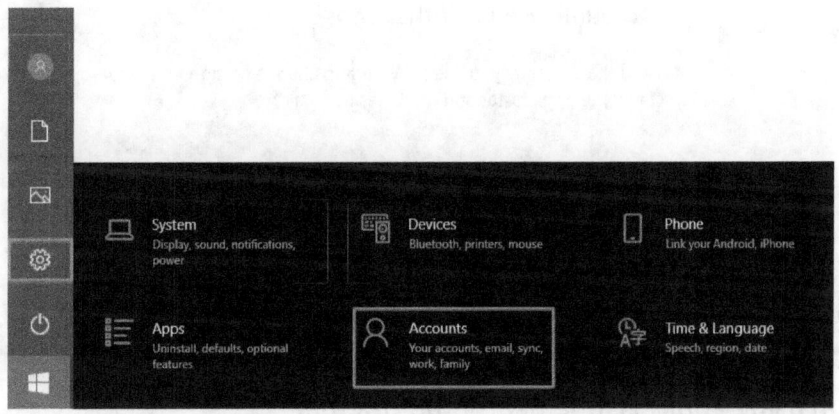

2. 2. Click on **Email and accounts.**

3. 3. Select **add a Microsoft account**.

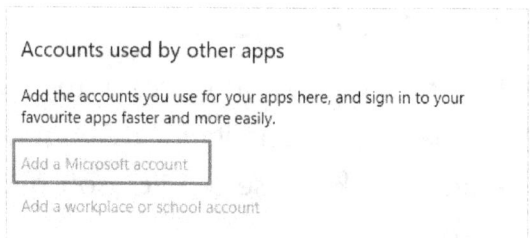

You can also add a workplace or school account by clicking on the link provided.

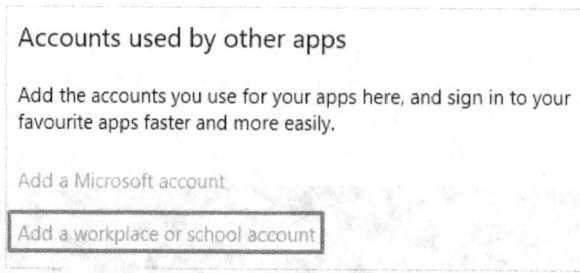

To log in to an existing account;
1. Click on **Add a Microsoft account**.
2. Sign in using your existing username or email

3.2 FAMILY ACCOUNTS AND PARENTAL CONTROL

Due to the rise in social media platforms, it is necessary to safeguard your children from the negative impacts of the internet. You can make use of Parental control options provided by Microsoft windows to monitor and control their activities. You can keep track of activities such as hours spent on the internet, browsing, and download history.

To activate the parental control settings;

1. Go to settings > Account
2. Select the **'Family & other users'** option on the left side to create a new Microsoft account.

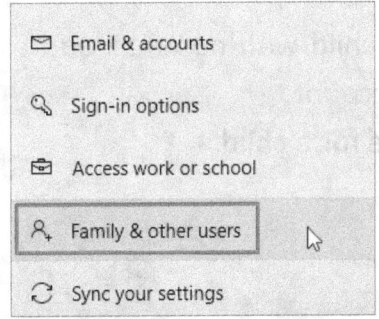

3. Click on **'Add a family member'**.

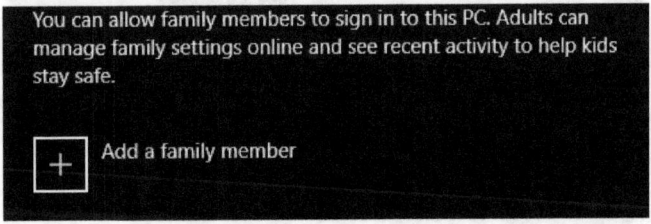

A new page will be created, prompting you to add someone.

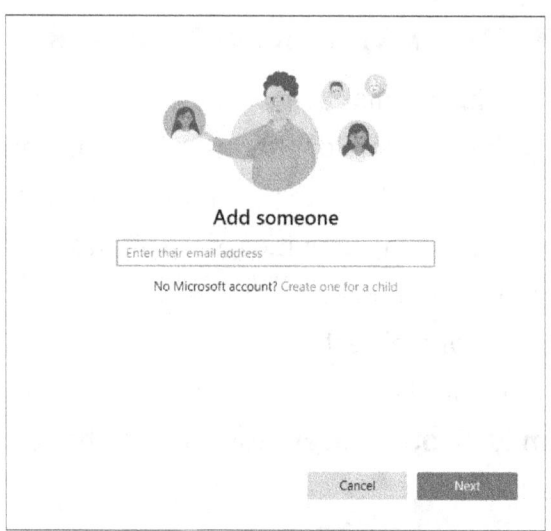

Since you are adding a child with no email address, use the link underneath to create a new Microsoft account.

4. Click on **Create one for a child.**

5. From the create account page, enter the preferred email you want to use

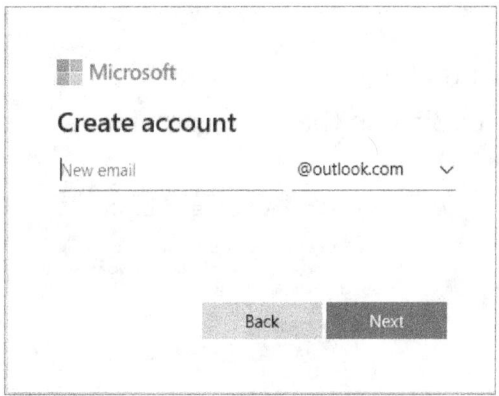

6. Click **Next**
7. Enter your preferred password in the space provided

8. On the next page, Enter the first and the last name.

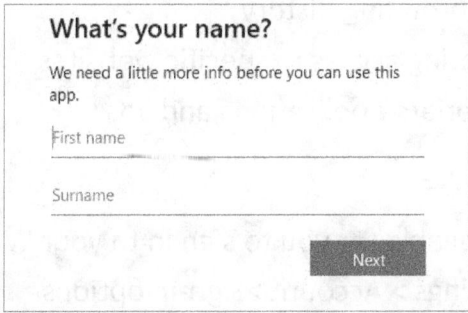

9. Click on **Next**
10. Select your Country/Region
11. Enter the Date of Birth in the space provided.

12. Click on **Next** to finish creating the account.

You should receive a notification that the new account has joined your family as a child.

To gain complete control of your child's activities, click the **'manage family settings online** link.

You will now have an opportunity to manage your family's activities such as;
- Monitoring their browsing history
- Blocking and granting access to specific websites
- Blocking inappropriate applications and ads

3.3 SIGN-IN OPTIONS

Several options are available for you to sign in to your Windows 10 device.
- Go to Start > settings > Account >Sign-in options

You can make use of the available sign-in options to log in to your device. To show your account clearly on the screen while signing in, you can toggle on the privacy section on the Sign-in options page.

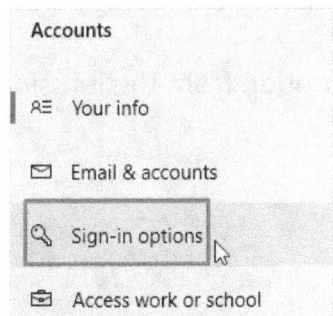

3.4 PERSONALIZING YOUR LOCK SCREEN

To access your lock screen;
1. Click on the start button or press the Windows logo key on your keyboard.
2. Right-click on your account and click **Lock**.

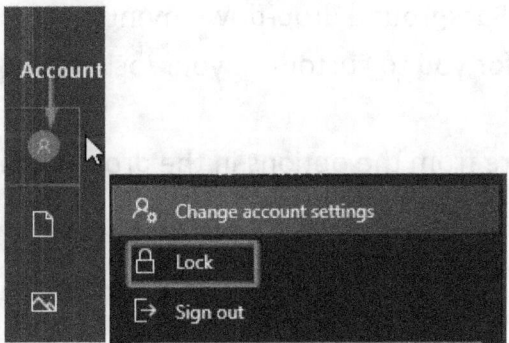

To customize your lock screen settings;
1. Right-click on the desktop and click on **Personalize**

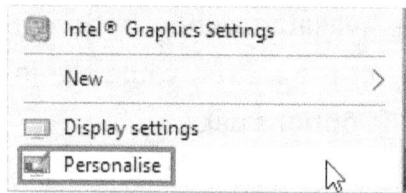

2. Select the **lock screen** option from the left side of the screen.

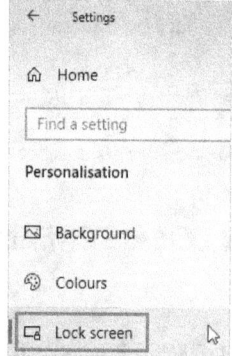

You can change the lock screen background image by selecting any of the three options listed in the Background drop-down menu.

There is an option for you to customize your lock screen using any picture of your choice.

1. Click on **Picture** from the options in the drop-down menu.

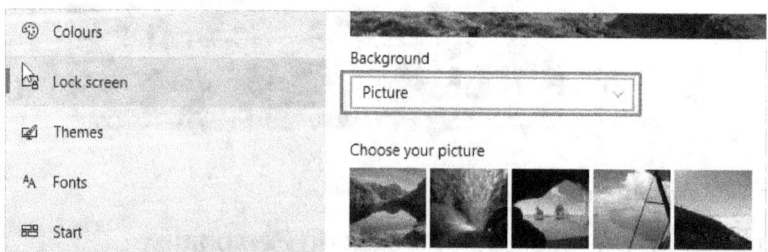

2. Click on **Browse** to access your saved folders.

3. Select your preferred image
4. Click on '**Choose picture**' to apply the image to your lock screen.

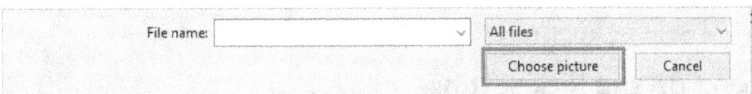

You can also make use of the slideshow option for your lock screen. However, there is a need to create a separate folder consisting of all the desired pictures for the slideshow.

To use Slideshow for your lock screen;

1. Select Slideshow from the Background drop-down.

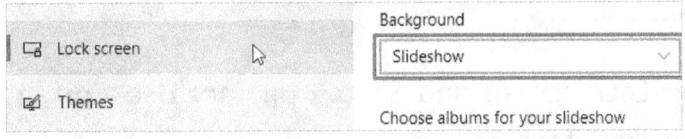

2. Click on '**Add a folder**'.

3. Select your preferred folder containing the pictures to be used for your lock screen slide show.

You can select the application that displays quick status on the lock screen by clicking on the plus (+) tile shown in the '**choose which app show quick status in the lock screen**' option.

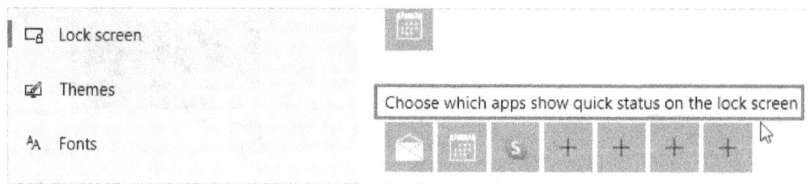

3.4.1 CORTANA LOCK SCREEN SETTINGS

As a user, you can use Cortana even when your device is locked.
From the lock screen settings;
1. Click on **Cortana lock settings**.

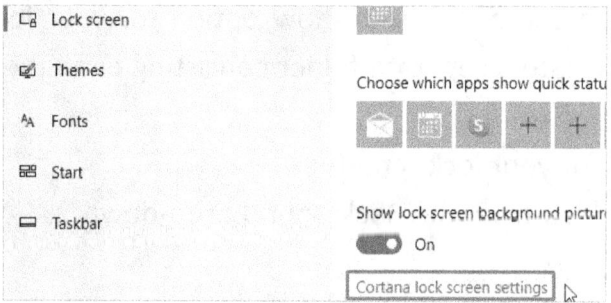

2. Go to the Lock screen and Switch on the '**Use Cortana even when my device is locked'** toggle.

There is a checkbox under the Talk to Cortana settings where you can permit Cortana to access some of the computer's features when your device is locked.

28

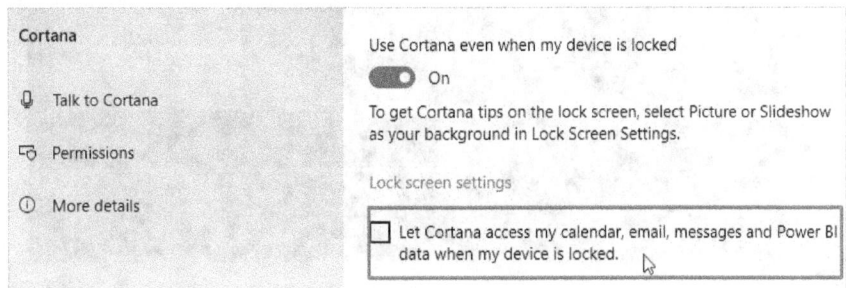

3.5 CUSTOMIZING THE BACKGROUND SETTINGS

You can personalize your desktop background by using any picture of your choice. To change your background settings;

Right-click on your desktop area and click on **Personalize** to access the background settings page.

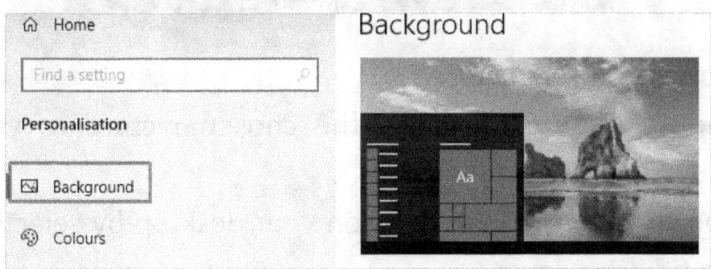

You can select any of the three options from the Background drop-down menu.

3.5.1 PICTURE

Selecting '**picture**' from the drop-down allows you to customize your background image using any picture of your choice. To use a picture as your desktop background image;

1. Select **Picture** from the Background drop-down menu.

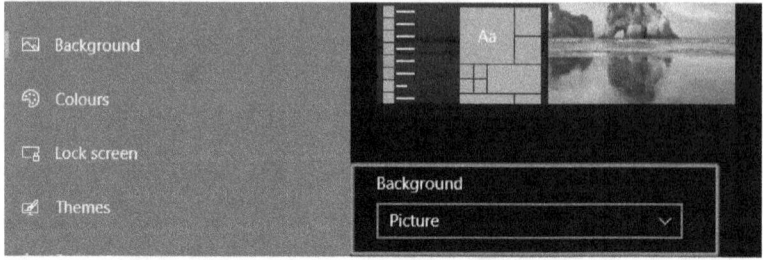

2. Click on **Browse** to choose your picture.

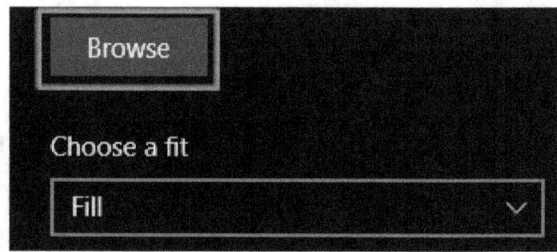

3. Select your preferred picture.
4. Click **Choose picture** to assign the chosen picture as your background image.

You can customize how the image fits on your desktop by selecting from the list in the 'Choose a fit' drop-down.

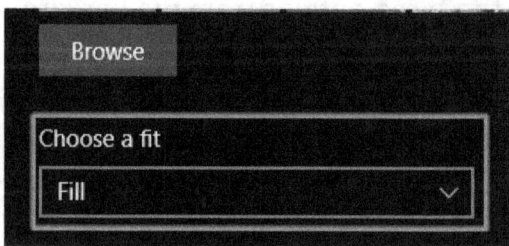

3.5.2 SLIDESHOW

You may also prefer to use a slideshow.
1. Select Slideshow from the Background Menu drop-down

2. Click on **Browse**, then

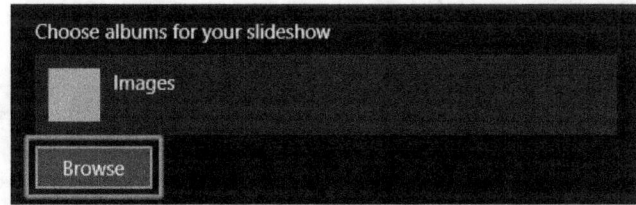

3. Select the folder containing only the pictures you want to use for your slideshow.
4. After making this selection, select **Choose this folder** to start using the slide show for your Background.

Windows has made it possible to customize the time it takes pictures in the slideshow to display. You can select your preferred time from the '**Change picture every'** drop-down menu.

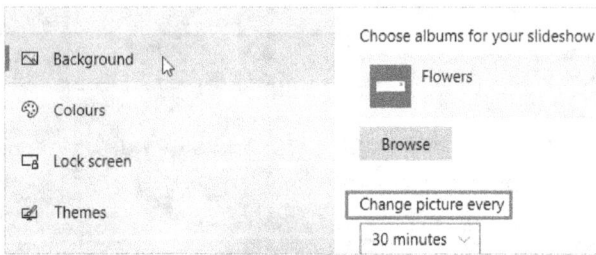

You can shuffle the pictures to follow a random pattern, and you can choose to use slide show when you are on battery power. The toggles provided for the stated options can be switched on or off based on your preference.

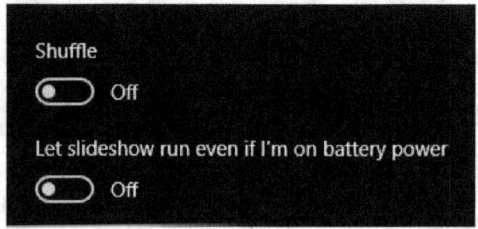

3.5.3 SOLID COLOR

The third option from the Background drop-down menu is the Solid color
1. Select **Solid Color** the listed options in the Background menu
2. Select your preferred color from the list provided in the '**Choose your background color.**'

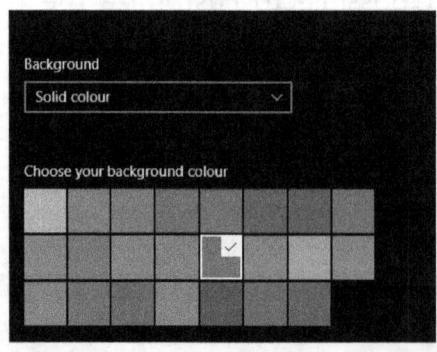

If you do not feel like using any of the listed solid colors, you may choose to customize your color by mixing different colors to create a unique background color for your desktop background. To do this;
1. Click on the **Custom color**.

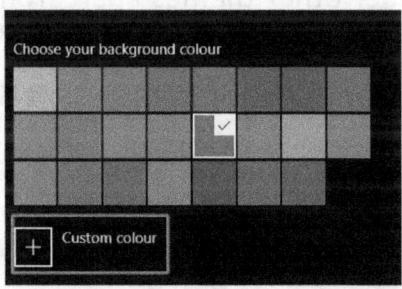

2. Click anywhere within the area to select your preferred color.

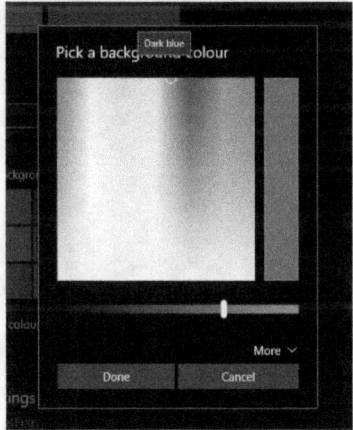

3. Adjust the brightness using the settings provided underneath
4. Click on **Done** when you have successfully customized your desired color.

3.6   CHOOSING THE RIGHT THEMES FOR YOUR WINDOWS 10

Windows theme is divided into four main categories (Background, Color, Sounds, and Mouse cursor). To customize the theme settings;

1. Go to Start > Settings > Personalization
2. Click on **Themes**
3. Click on any of the four theme options to customize the settings
4. Click on **Save theme** to apply the changes

You may want to consider other themes apart from those available within your device. To do this;

- Click on the '**Get more themes in Microsoft Store**' link to download more themes.

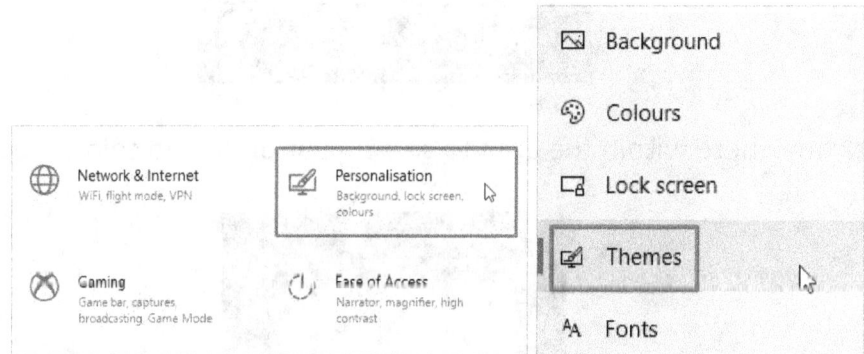

SECTION FOUR - USING THE WINDOWS 10 SETTINGS

4.1 DATE AND TIME SETTINGS

To adjust or set the date and time on your device;
1. Right-click on the date on the taskbar area.
2. Click on **Adjust date/ time.**

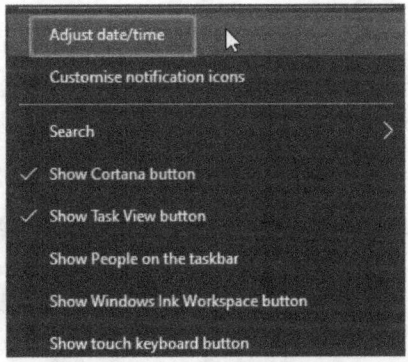

Alternatively;
1. Go to Start > Settings > Time and Language
2. Click on '**Date and time.**'

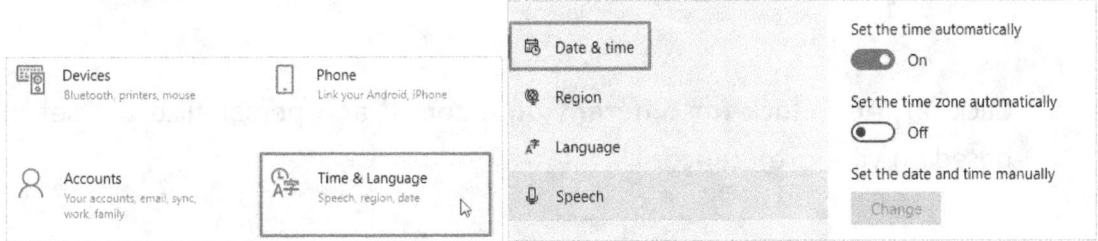

To automatically set the time, toggle on the '**Set the time automatically**' switch. If you have got any reason to set the time manually, toggle off the switch and use the **change** button in the **Set the date and time manually**. You can also set your time zone automatically using the **Set the time zone automatically** toggle switch.

If you prefer to set the time zone manually, toggle off the switch and use the Time zone drop-down menu.

To further personalize your time and date, use the links in the related settings.

4.2 ADDITIONAL CLOCK AND REGION SETTINGS

Do you know that you can set clocks of different time zones in addition to the time in your region?

The setting is possible on Windows 10. Let us assume that you are attending a virtual meeting scheduled to hold in a different location. You can use the additional clock feature to set the time in the region.

To customize the Additional Clock and Region settings;

1. Go to Start > Setting > Time and Language > Date and time settings

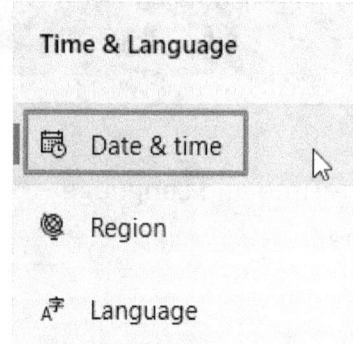

2. Click on '**Add Clock for different time zones**' and personalize the settings based on your preference.

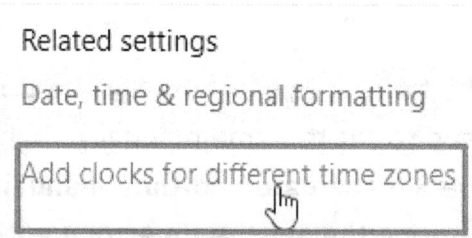

4.3 SYSTEM SETTINGS

4.3.1 DISPLAY SETTINGS

The display settings allow you to adjust display options such as text, brightness, color, and overall appearance of the contents of your screen.

You can access the display settings from the desktop or the system settings.

To access from your desktop;
- Right-click on your desktop and click on display settings.

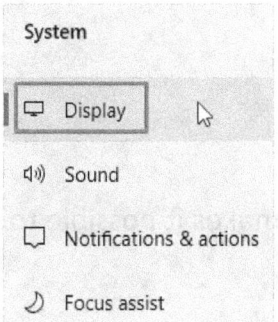

➢ USING THE NIGHT LIGHT

The Night Light is a built-in feature in Windows 10 that comes up when the day gets darker or at night. It helps to reduce the blue light emitted by the screen, which keeps the user awake.

- Click on **Night light settings** to customize Night light.

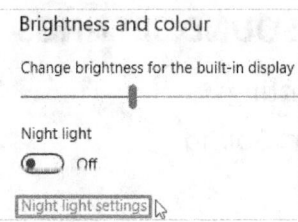

To use the nightlight tool, turn it on using the button provided.

You can manually adjust the Night light strength based on your preference. To schedule the Night light, use the toggle switch provided.

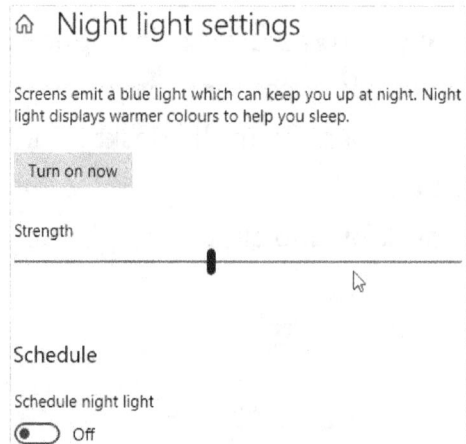

The **scale and layout setting** makes it possible to customize the display resolution and orientation.

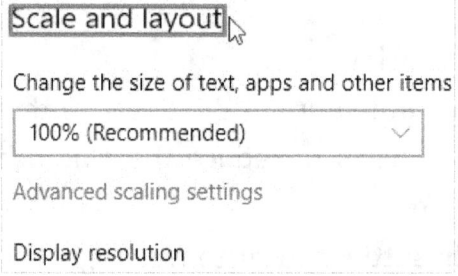

4.3.2 CUSTOMIZING THE SOUND SETTINGS

To personalize your sound settings;
Go to Start > Settings >System >Sound

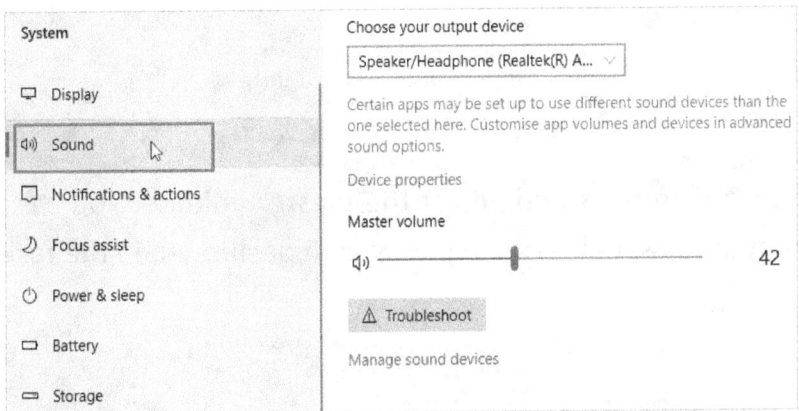

From the sound settings, you can use the **device properties** link to rename and disable your speaker or headphone, select the special sound and adjust the balance.

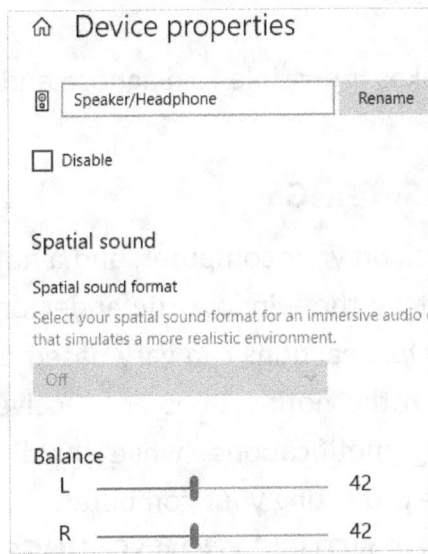

You can further personalize your sound in the device properties using the **Additional device properties** link.

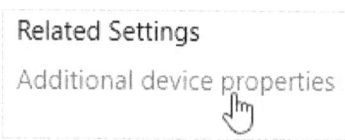

Go back to Sound settings and adjust the **master volume**. You can as well make this adjustment in the speaker/ headphone icon positioned in the taskbar.

The '**Manage sound devices link'** allows for disabling and testing the output devices while also making it possible to disable the input sound devices.

You can make use of the advanced sound options to further customize your sound devices.

Troubleshoot button makes it possible to diagnose and fix issues with your sound device.

4.3.3 NOTIFICATIONS SETTINGS

Imagine performing a task on your computer, and a notification pops up to notify you of a scan carried out by the windows defender or to inform you about the latest windows updates. Our reactions can vary based on individual preference or the condition under which the notifications are received. For example, you may want to stop receiving notifications while holding meetings or making presentations that involve projecting your computer.

> **CUSTOMIZING YOUR NOTIFICATION SETTINGS**

Notifications updates in windows are beneficial as they can present us with helpful information on critical system and security updates for the overall health of our computer. However, it is more likely that some users prefer not to receive notifications. To stop getting notifications;

1. Go to Start > Notification and actions settings.

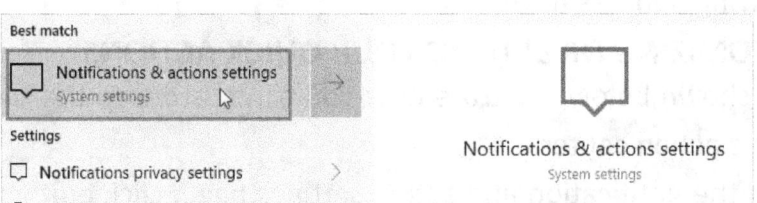

2. Toggle off the '**Get notifications from apps and other senders**' under **Notifications** to stop receiving new notifications on your computer.

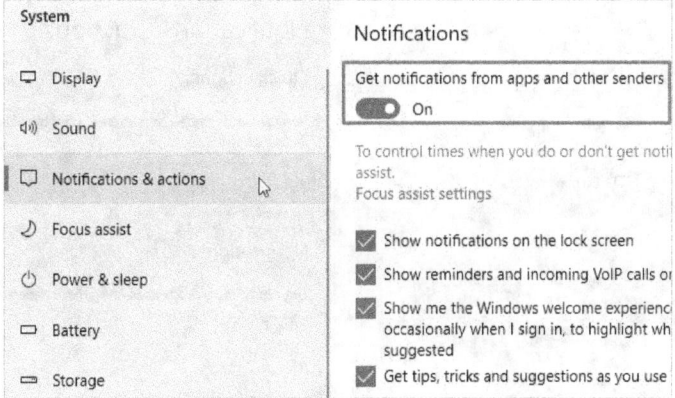

To select or customize which application sends you notifications
- Scroll down to '**Get notifications from these apps**

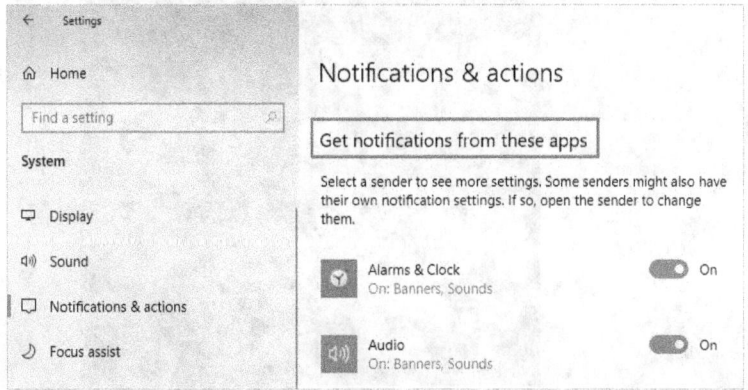

- You can switch off the toggle for any of the listed applications to stop receiving updates from them.

➢ **CUSTOMIZING OR EDITING YOUR QUICK ACTIONS**

The steps shown below illustrate how you can customize the tiles on your quick actions in the action center.

1. From the notification and action settings page, click **edit your quick actions** link.

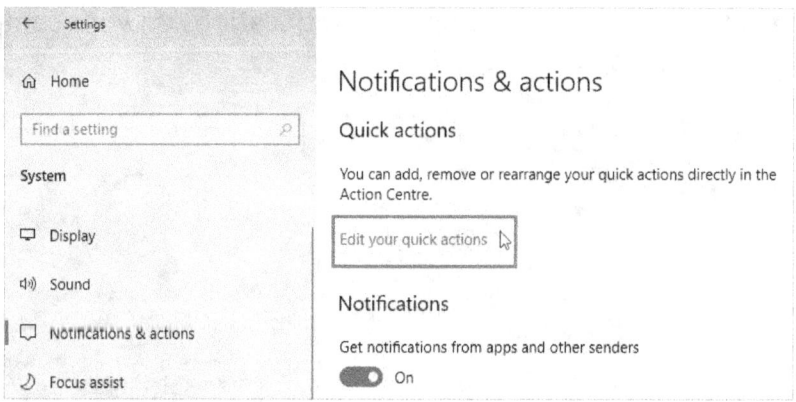

2. Click on the unpin icon in the top right corner of your chosen tile to remove it from the list.

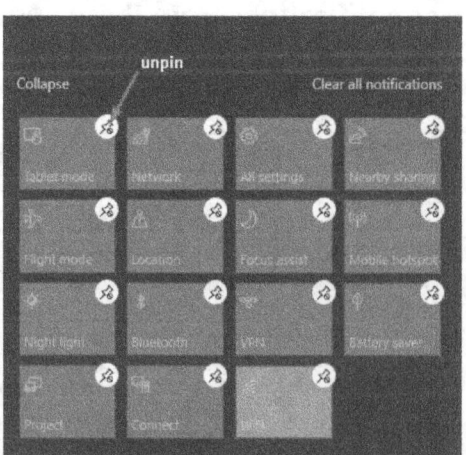

You can add more tiles by clicking on **Add icon** in the action center.

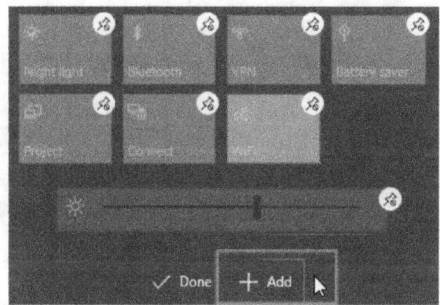

> **FLIGHT MODE**

Flight mode, also known as the airplane mode, disables your Wi-Fi, internet, or Bluetooth connections. If you are using a touch screen device, you can access the flight mode by flipping your hand from the right side of your screen. You can also access flight mode by clicking on the action center icon or pressing the Windows key + A on your keyboard.

To turn on flight mode;
1. Press Windows key + A
2. Click on the **flight mode** tile to turn it on. Doing this will enable the airplane mode and disable any internet connection.

Click on the enabled flight mode to turn it off and reactivate your network connections

4.3.4 USING THE FOCUS ASSIST

See yourself as a data analyst who just resumed back to work after a long vacation. While trying to concentrate on the work at hand, several notifications start showing up on your screen. To help you avoid distractions and allow you to focus more on your tasks, windows 10 has a built-in feature known as focus assist.

To use and customize the focus assist settings;
- Go to Start > Settings > System > Focus assist

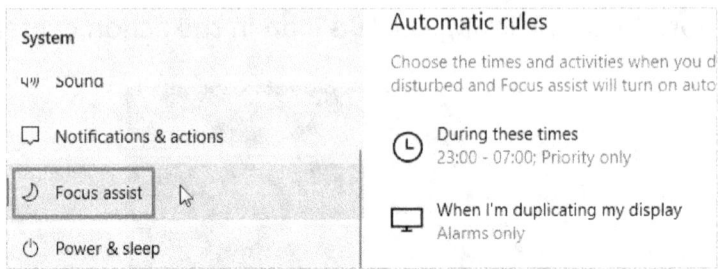

The first three options in the Focus assist allow you to choose the notifications you can see on your screen. You can further customize your priority list by clicking on **Customize your priority** link.

Use Automatic rules toggles to turn on focus assist when performing some specific tasks.

4.3.5 NEARBY SHARING

With Nearby sharing, you can share files or documents with other devices within your workplace or home using Bluetooth or Wi-Fi.

To turn on your nearby sharing;

Go to Action center> Nearby sharing

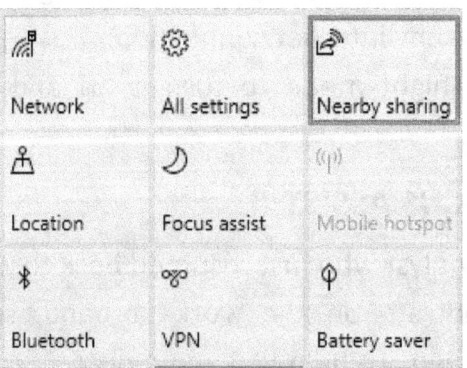

Alternatively;

Go to Start > settings > System > Shared experiences

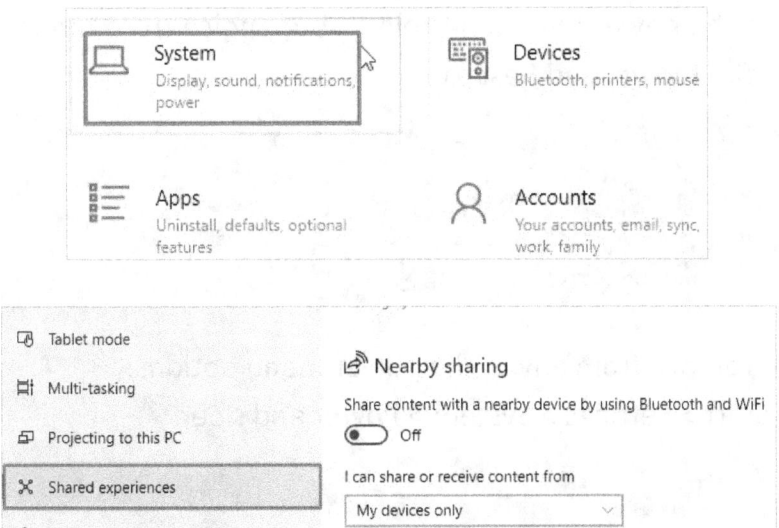

To start sharing, turn on the **nearby sharing** toggle.

Use the '**I can share or receive content from**' drop-down menu to choose whether you can share and receive from your device only or everyone nearby.

4.3.6 POWERING OPTIONS FOR YOUR DEVICE

Assuming you have been working on your device for over three hours and it's time for you to rest, intending to continue from where you stopped. You might want to put your computer to sleep, knowing that your files are still opened. On the other hand, if you feel you have completed your tasks and it is time for you to go to bed, you can consider shutting down your computer. Shutting it down will stop all the applications from running and will save your battery power.

Also, think of a situation when using your device, and a notification pops up for an important update. For most updates, you need to restart your system after the installation.

To access and use the right power option;
1. Click on the start button or press the Windows logo key on your keyboard.

2. Click on the power menu and select your choice from the available options (Sleep, Shutdown, and Restart).

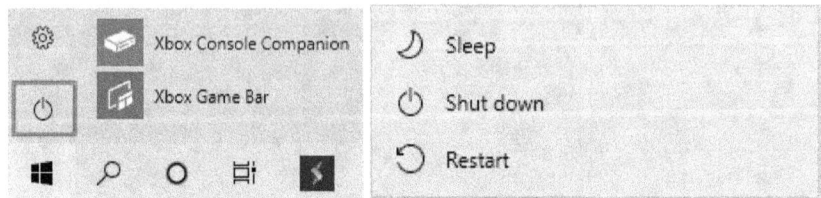

To add to or remove from any of the power menu options;
1. Go to Start > Settings > System > Power and sleep

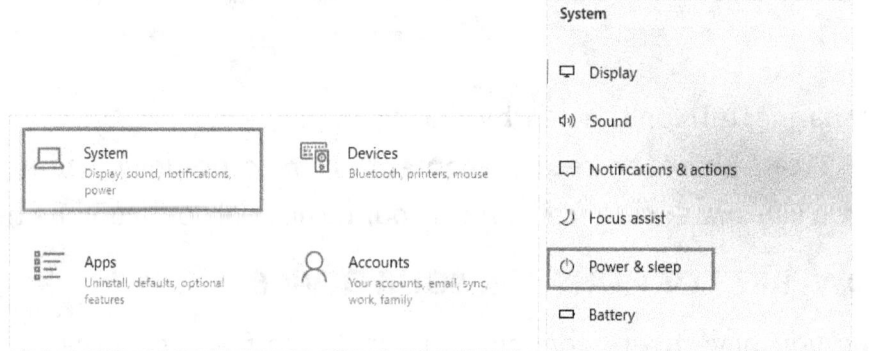

2. Click on the **Additional power settings** link.

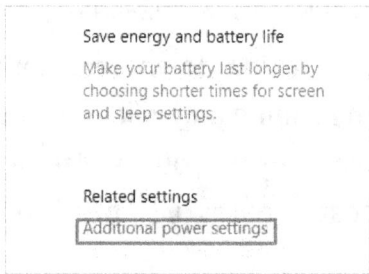

3. From the options in the control panel, click on '**Choose what the power button does**.'

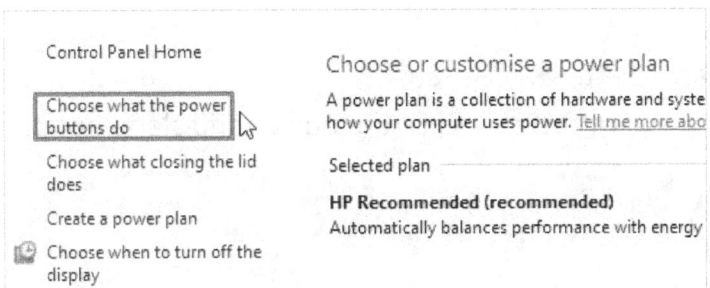

4. From the Shut-down settings, check on the '**hibernate**' box to add the option to the power menu.

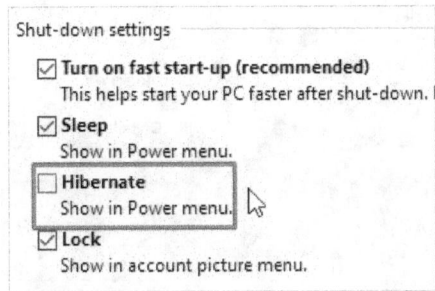

> ## CUSTOMIZING YOUR POWER OPTIONS

Some of the installed applications and features on your computer tend to affect the power or drain the battery faster than usual when they are active. Windows has options for users to customize their power settings.

To customize your power-saving options;

Using the search box, Go to power and sleep settings.

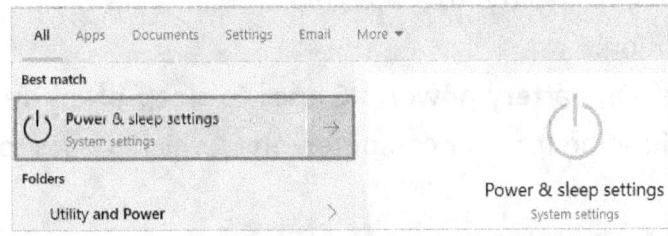

Alternatively;
1. Go to Start > Settings > System
2. From the system settings, click the power and sleep option.

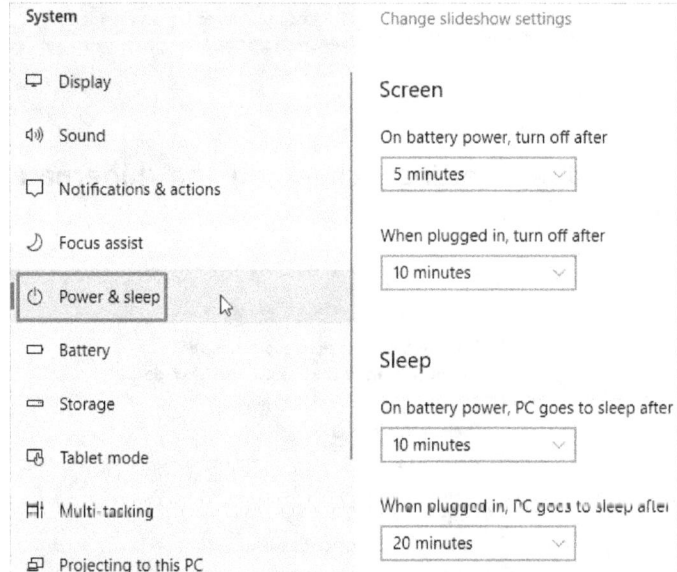

As the name implies, **'Power and sleep'** is divided into the Screen option and the sleep option.

To utilize the screen option for saving your battery power;

Use the **'On battery power, turn off after'** drop-down menu to set the on-time for the screen.

You can use the **'When plugged in, turn off after'** button to set the screen on time duration when connected to a charger.

For the sleep option;

You can use the **'On battery power, PC goes to sleep after'** drop-down menu to set the on-time duration for your computer, after which it goes to sleep.

Also, make use of the '**when plugged in, PC goes to sleep after**' drop-down menu to set the time required for the computer to be on when it is not being used before it goes to sleep. However, it only applies when the system is plugged in.

You can further personalize your power settings from the related settings option.

Click on the '**Additional power settings**' to access the power options page.

You can customize what the power button does when pressed by clicking on the '**Choose what the power buttons do**' option.

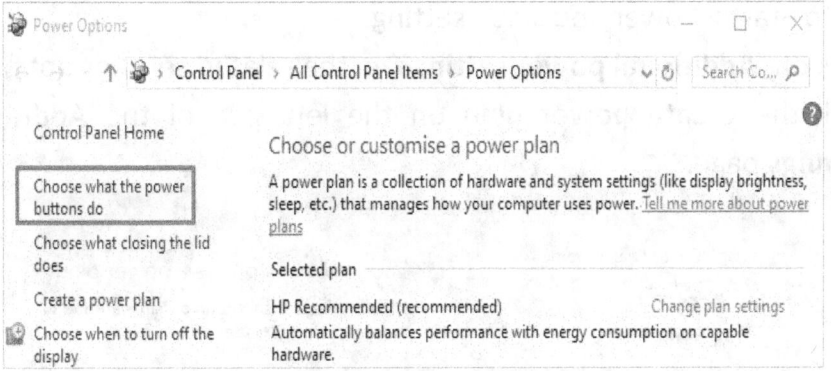

Select from the drop-down menu, what happens when you press the power button when the computer is on **battery mode** and when it is **plugged in**.

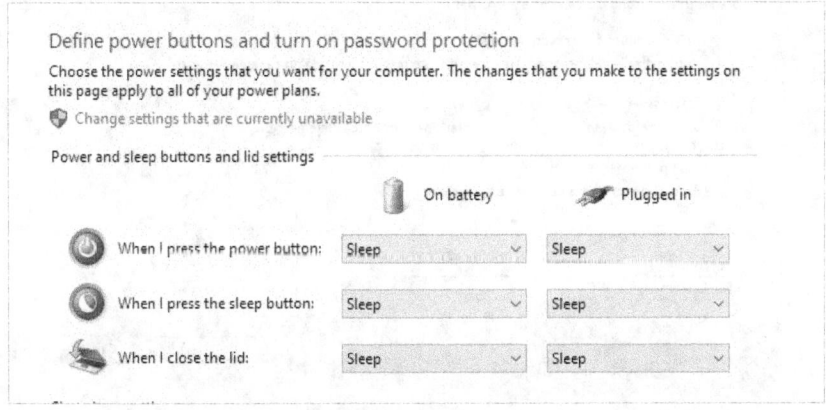

You can also choose what happens to your computer when you close the lid and when the sleep button is pressed using the drop-down menu for the two options.

➢ CREATING A POWER PLAN

To control the total amount of power consumed by your device's applications and tools, use the default power plan previously set on your computer and which can be customized based on your preference.

To customize your power plan;
1. Go to Start > Power and sleep settings
2. Click on '**Additional power settings**' in the related settings option.
3. Click the **Create power plan** on the left side of the **Additional Power Settings** page.

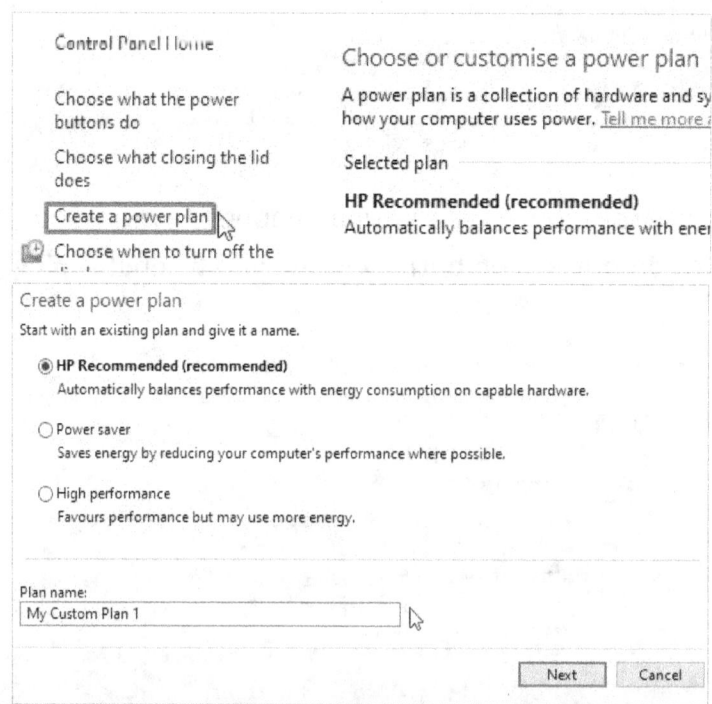

You will observe that the default or existing plan is **HP recommended**. Other options are provided, which include Power saver and High-performance options. However, you may choose to create your power plan by doing the following;

Type your preferred Plan name in the '**Plan name**' box and then click Next.

The '**Edit plan settings**' page is where you can customize the settings for your new plan.

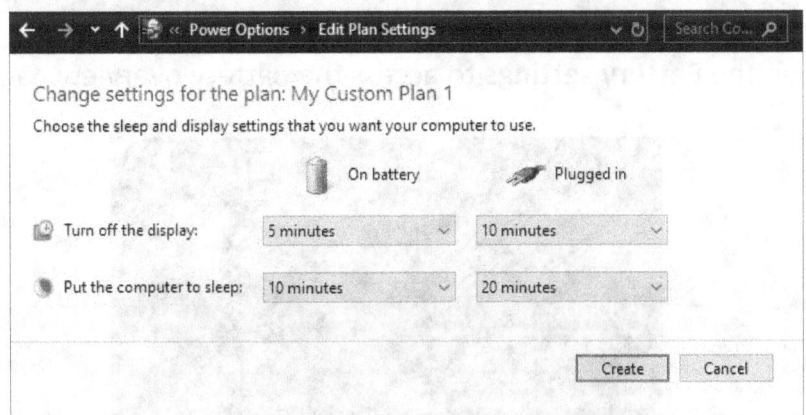

Use the drop-down menu to set the time to turn off the display and put the computer to sleep when plugged in and on battery mode.

Click the **Create** button to set up your new Power plan

4.3.7 CUSTOMIZING YOUR BATTERY SETTINGS

You can monitor which applications affect your battery life by carrying out the following;

1. Click the Battery icon on the taskbar to see the percentage of total power left. Here, you can adjust the settings for best performance or best battery life.

2. Click on the **Battery settings** to access the battery overview page.

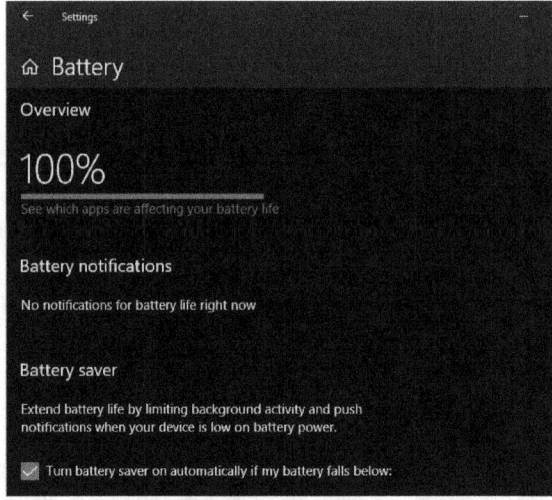

Click on '**See which apps are affecting your battery life**' to monitor your battery usage by the applications being run on your computer.

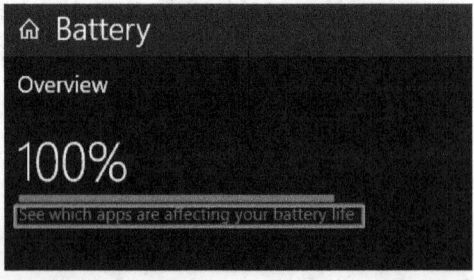

You can further increase your battery life by using the **battery saver** options on the Battery settings page. There is an option to fix or adjust when the battery saver mode is turned on due to limited battery power.

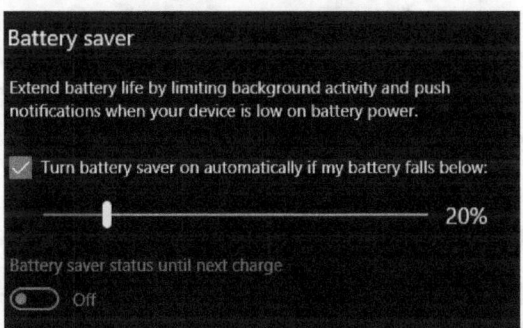

To lower the screen brightness while the battery is in battery saver mode, click the checkbox provided below the battery saver option.

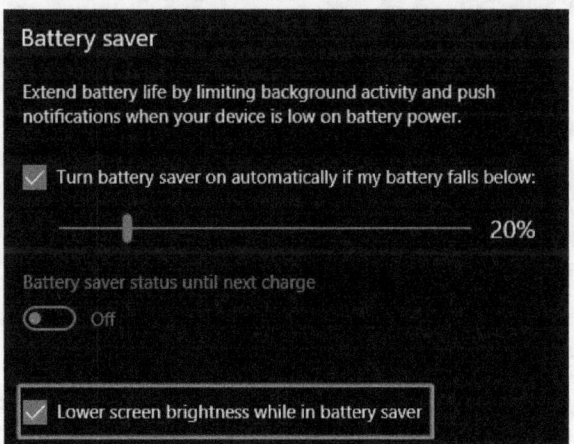

4.4   EASE OF ACCESS SETTINGS

Windows ease of access is a helpful tool that makes the device easier and more convenient to use for everyone. Its interface has been subdivided into three major categories; Vision, Hearing, and Interaction.

➤ VISION

The vision part helps to customize the appearance, texts, and themes of the computer screen. It can be specifically beneficial for users with eye defects and reading difficulties.

➤ HEARING

The hearing option is set up to help users with hearing issues. It detects and converts audio into visual displays.

➤ INTERACTION

On the other hand, the interaction option is another useful tool to ease how the user relates with the device and applications. It may help users who need to limit the extent of using their hands to navigate through their devices.

To open the ease of access settings;

1. Type Ease of Access in the Search box
2. Click on Ease of Access brightness settings

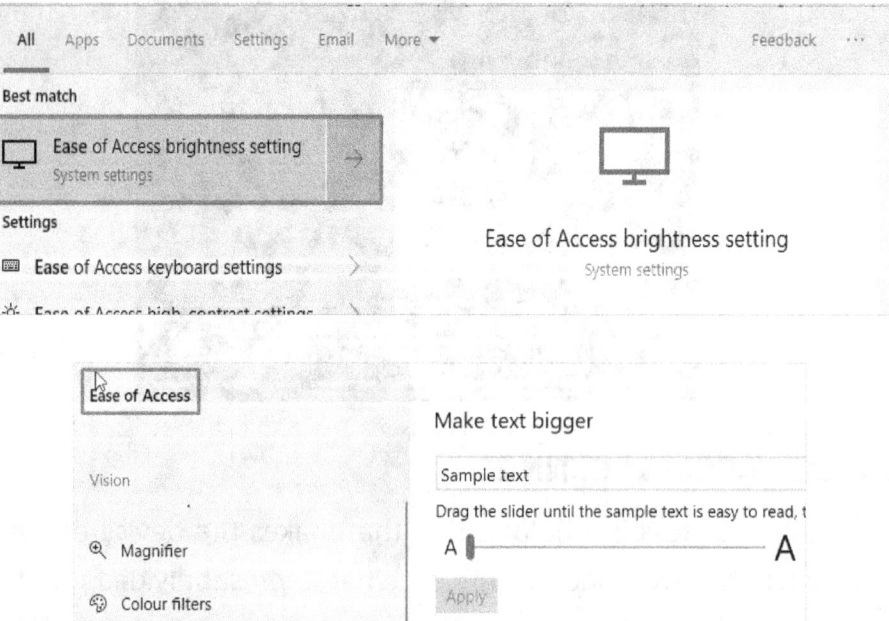

4.4.1 DISPLAY SETTINGS

➢ MAKE TEXT BIGGER

Windows have made provision to customize displayed texts on the screen, making it less difficult to read.

To customize your font or text size;
1. Go to Start > Settings > Ease of Access
2. Click on the **Display option**

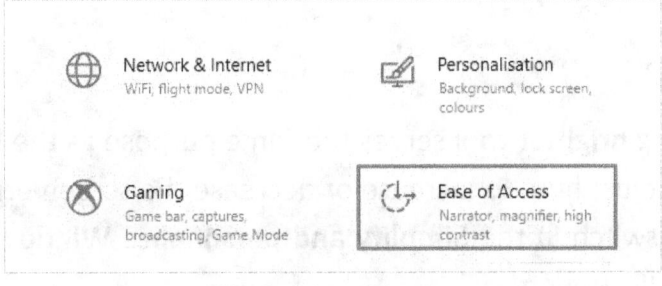

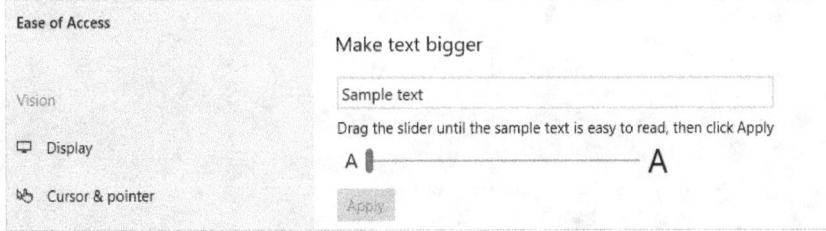

You can adjust the text size by dragging towards left or right while observing the changes made from the **Sample text** in the box. When you have set your preferred text size;
Click on **Apply** to effect the change.

➢ MAKE EVERYTHING BIGGER

Using the '**make everything bigger**' option will make everything on the screen looks bigger than the original size.

Click on the '**Change the size of apps and text on other displays**' link to make further changes.

By clicking on this link, you can personalize different settings, such as screen brightness and color.

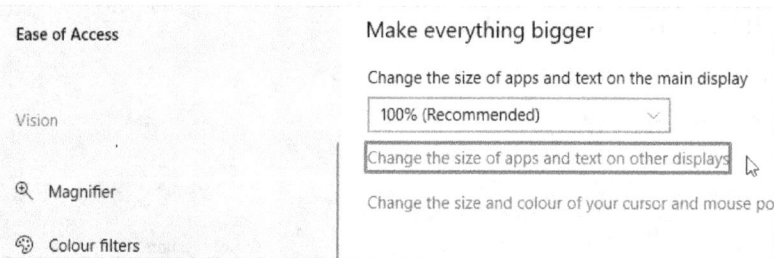

Make everything brighter tool serves the same purpose as the brightness icon on your keyboard. Adjust here to increase or decrease the screen brightness.

Use the toggle switch in the **Simplify and personalize Windows** option to make your preferred adjustments.

4.4.2 CURSOR AND POINTER

As a user, you may strain your eyes every time your cursor is being used. Windows has made it easy to adjust the pointer's size and customize its appearance.

1. From the Ease of access page, Go to **Cursor and pointer.**

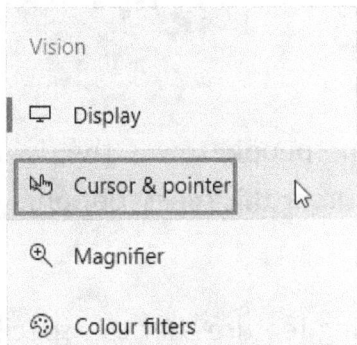

2. Adjust the size of the pointer from '**Change pointer size.**'

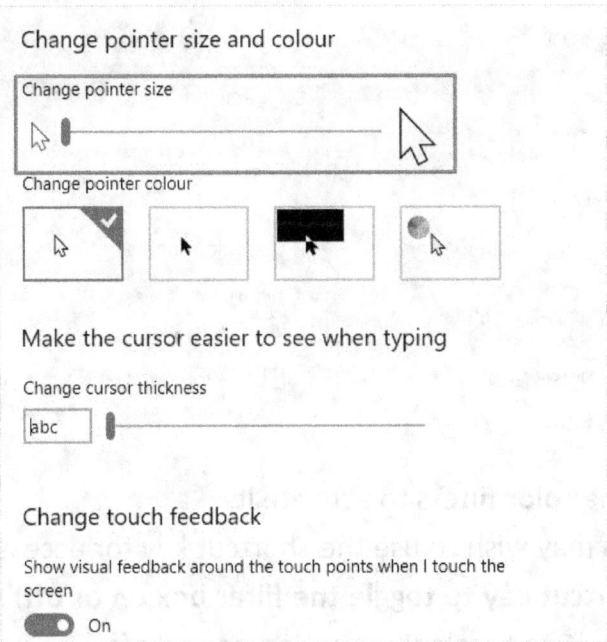

   To change the color of your pointer, use the customization options provided in the '**Change the pointer color.**'

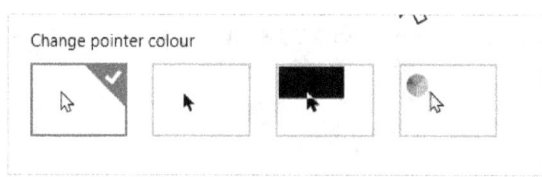

It could be difficult for some people to see the default cursor thickness to make changes using the '**Change cursor thickness**' option.

4.4.3 COLOR FILTERS

The Color filter is an amazing feature that can specifically help people with color blindness. To access this page;
1. Go to Start > Ease of access > Color filters.

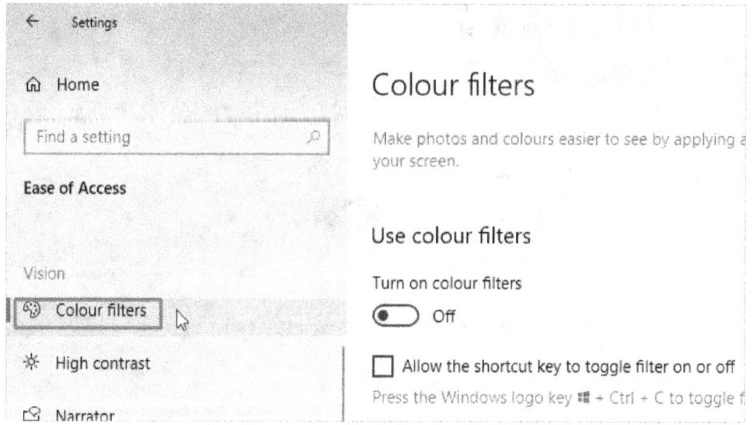

2. Toggle on the **color filters** to activate it.

Alternatively, you may wish to use the shortcut key for accessing this page. Check the '**Allow the shortcut key to toggle the filter box on or off**, then press Windows Logo key + Control + C to toggle filter option on and off.

You can select any of the listed color filter options (Inverted, Greyscale, and Greyscale inverted) to have a better view of the contents of your screen.

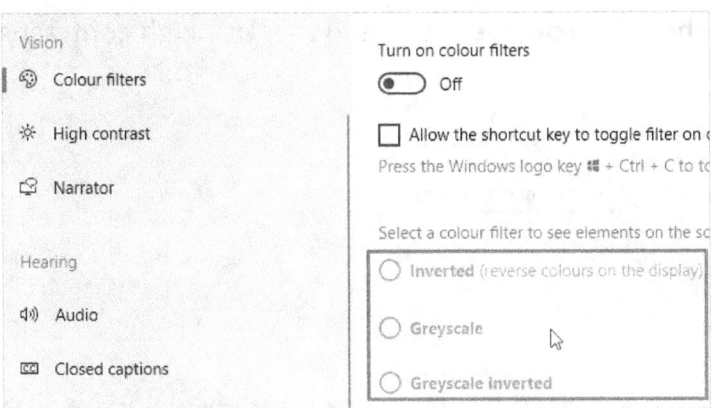

You can also select from the color blindness filter options to make the wheel colors more distinct.

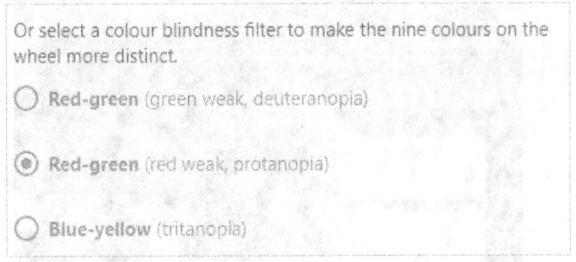

4.4.4 HIGH CONTRAST

The high contrast option makes it easier to see your texts and applications on your device. The idea here is to use high contrast colors, such as white texts on a black background or black texts on white background. To use the High contrast;
1. Go to Start > Ease of access > High contrast.

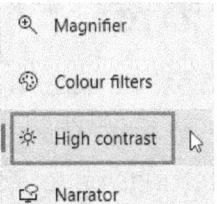

2. Turn on the '**high contrast**' toggle in the 'Use high contrast section.'

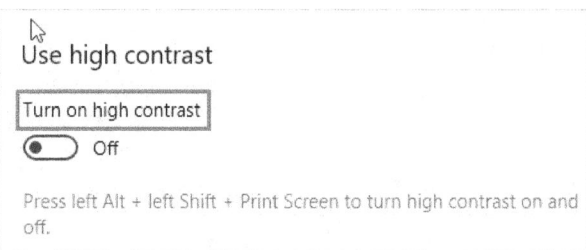

3. Choose your preferred theme in the list of available high contrast themes in the drop-down.

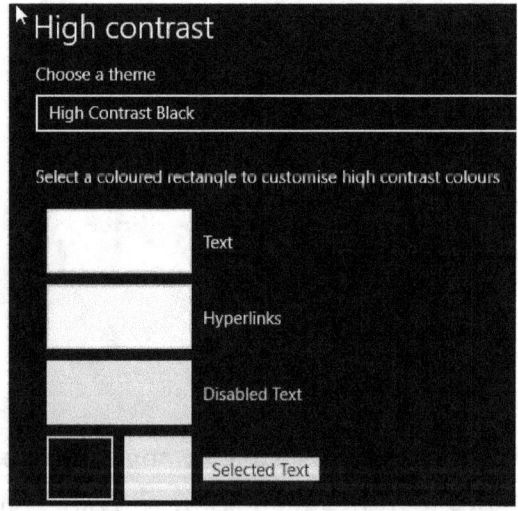

You can further personalize this feature by selecting a colored rectangle from the list provided—Click Apply to effect the changes.

4.4.5 USING WINDOWS NARRATOR

Windows narrator is also known as the screen reader. It is a tool that tells you or reads out what you have on the screen. There are several customization options available to you on the narrator settings page. To use the windows narrator;

1. Go to Start > Ease of access > Narrator.

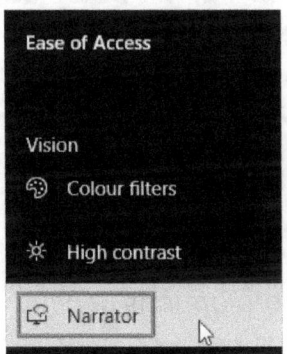

2. Use the toggle switch to turn on the narrator or
Press Windows Logo Key + Ctrl + Enter to turn on or off the narrator.

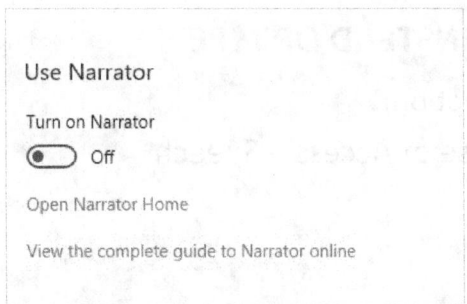

Use the **open narrator home** to gain more information about the narrator, its functions, and how to navigate it. Clicking on the link takes you to the welcome to narrator page. The page has five options; QuickStart, Narrator guide, What's new, settings, and Feedback. You can also use the link provided for **viewing the complete narrator guide online**.

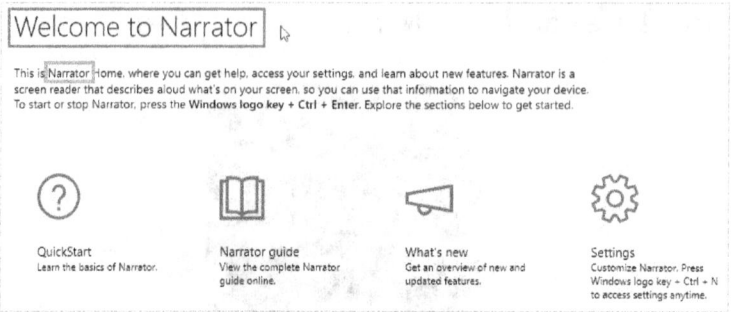

You can personalize your startup options depending on your personal preference. Personalizing the narrator's voice has made its usage more convenient and soothing because you can control your preferred accents. By adjusting the speed, voice pitch, it feels better when you listen to the narrator. There other customization options available in the narrator settings.

4.4.6 SPEECH: TALK INSTEAD OF TYPE

To access the speech option;
3. Go to Start > Ease of Access > Speech

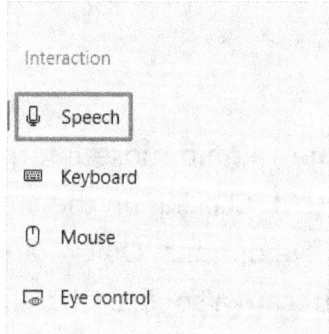

> ➢ **TALK INSTEAD OF TYPE**

This feature is helpful if you do not want to type with your keyboard. You can use the dictation option to type by just reading out for your device to type. Dictating your words will not only reduce the stress of typing; it will also help you to type faster.

Using the Cortana option: What if you want to know about weather conditions in some locations to prioritize your outings. While you are connected to the internet, you can ask Cortana to do the work for you without undergoing the stress of searching with your keyboard. You can carry out other tasks with less stress by using the Cortana app.

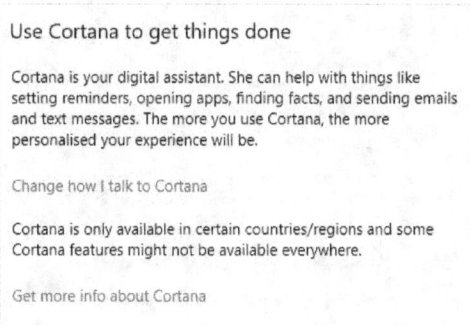

You can toggle on the speech recognition or press the Windows logo key + Ctrl + S to turn the speech recognition on or off. You can further customize the speech settings by using the related settings option provided.

Use Windows Logo key + H to start dictation.

4.4.7 KEYBOARD

The keyboard option in the interaction section makes it easier to type with your device and ease keyboard shortcuts. You can save the stress of typing with your physical keyboard by using the built-in on-screen keyboard app on your device. To use the on-screen keyboard;

1. Go to Start > Ease of Access > Keyboard.

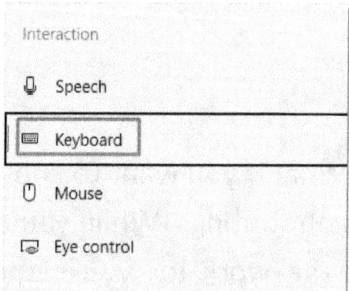

2. Toggle on the '**Use the On-Screen Keyboard**' or Press Windows logo key + Ctrl + O.

Using Sticky keys makes it convenient for you to press shortcut keys one at a time instead of pressing them together. For example, you can turn on the on-screen keyboard by pressing the Windows logo key, Ctrl key, and 'O' one at a time instead of pressing them altogether. Use the checkbox provided to customize your Sticky keys further.

You can play a sound when the caps Lock, Scroll Lock, or Num Lock is pressed by turning on the **Use Toggle Keys**. Use other personalization options in the keyboard settings based on your preference. To further customize the Keyboard option, use the links provided in the Related settings.

4.4.8 MOUSE

The mouse option of the Ease of access page makes it less stressful to see and control the mouse. You have the choice of controlling your mouse with a keypad.
1. In the search box, type and select **Settings**
2. Click on **Ease of Access**
3. Select the **Mouse** option

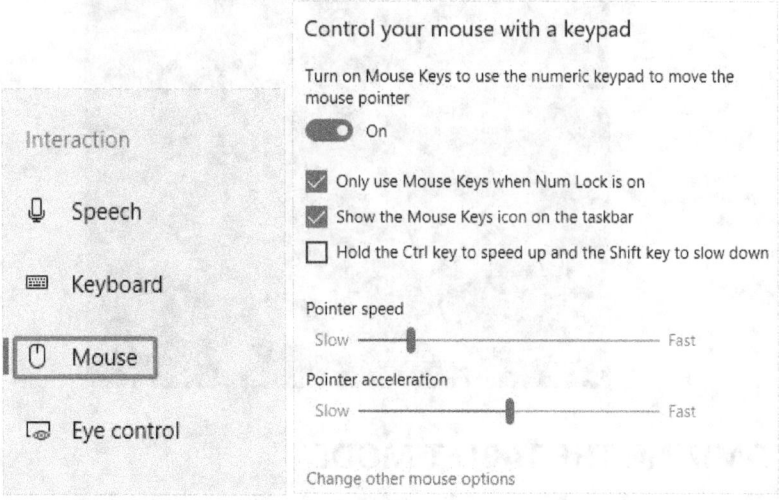

Turn on the Mouse keys and make other personalization such as setting the **pointer speed** and **acceleration** and using the provided checkboxes.

4.5 WORKING WITH TABLET MODE

Tablet mode is a tool that makes your work less stressful due to the touchscreen elements involved. When you switch to tablet mode, you can consider hiding your taskbar to get a full-screen start menu display. Then use your hand to scroll through the tiles in the start menu to select your preferred applications.

4.5.1 SWITCHING TO TABLET MODE

As a Windows 10 user, you may want to try this feature out and see if it is helpful. To switch on the tablet mode;
1. Click on the action center icon
2. Click on **Tablet mode** from the available tiles

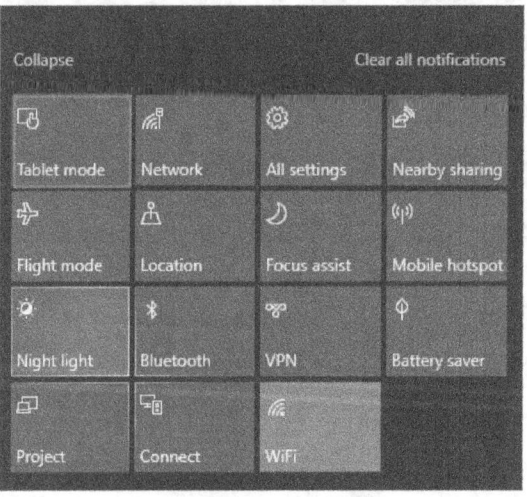

4.5.2 CUSTOMIZING THE TABLET MODE

1. Click on the Start button beside the search box or press the Windows logo key on your keyboard to open the start menu.
2. Click on **Settings**

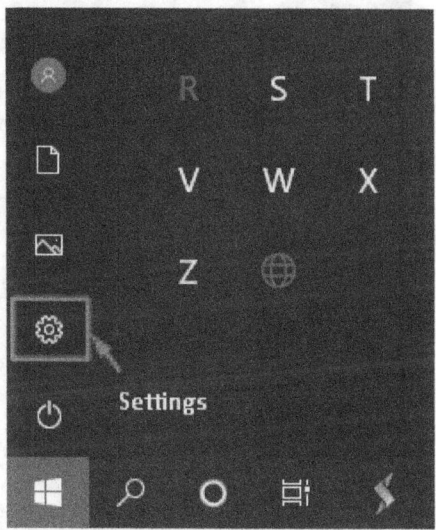

3. From the settings page, click on the **System** option.

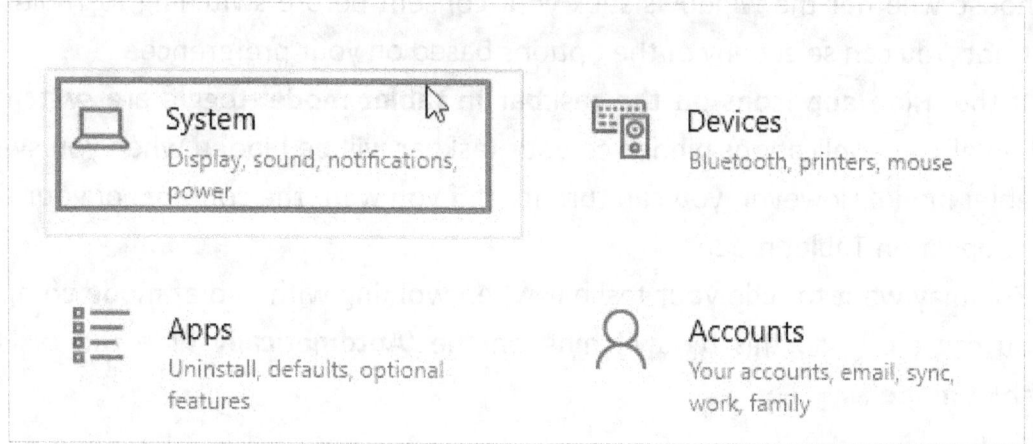

4. Click on **Tablet mode** from the list of system options to personalize your tablet mode settings.

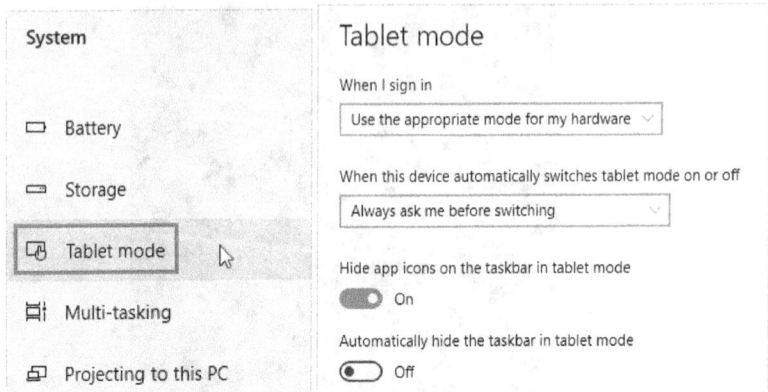

You can use the '**When I sign in**' menu to select if your computer starts with desktop or tablet mode when you log in to your device. You can select one of the three options from the drop-down based on your preference.

'**When this device automatically switches tablet mode on or off**' allows you to choose whether the windows seek your consent before switching to Tablet mode or not. You can select any of the options based on your preference.

If the '**Hide app icons on the taskbar in tablet mode**' toggle are switched on, then all the applications pinned to your taskbar will be hidden when you switch to Tablet mode. However, you can turn it off if you want the contents of your taskbar to appear on Tablet mode.

You may want to hide your taskbar when working with Tablet mode completely. You can easily do this by switching on the '**Automatically hide the taskbar in tablet mode**'.

4.5.3 SWITCHING FROM TABLET MODE TO DESKTOP MODE

To switch from Tablet mode back to Desktop mode;
1. Go to Action center> Tablet mode
2. Click on the active tablet mode to turn it off and switch back to desktop mode

SECTION FIVE - WINDOWS 10 APPLICATIONS

5.1 MICROSOFT STORE

Windows Store is Microsoft owned online marketplace or platform where users can download several contents such as games, music, videos, and other applications. You can compare the store to google play store for android phones and the app store for iPhones. The windows store is preinstalled on Windows 10 and can be found in the start menu. To access the Windows store;

1. Go to the Start menu by pressing the windows key or by clicking the start button.
2. From the app list, scroll down to the Microsoft store
3. Click on the Microsoft store application to access the store.

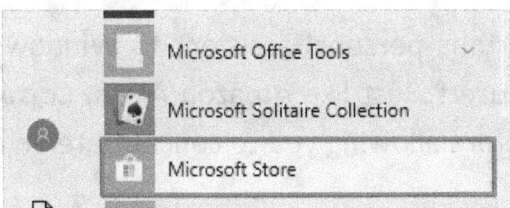

4. Type the specific application that you are looking for in the search bar

5. Click on your preferred application.
6. Select the GET or **Install** button to start downloading the application

The installation starts automatically after the application has been successfully downloaded. Check the notification area for notification showing that the application has been successfully installed.

5.2 USING THE CORTANA APP

The addition of Cortana personal assistant to Windows 10 has made life much easier for Windows users. Just like Amazon Alexa, Cortana can help you execute different tasks, therefore allowing you to concentrate on other work at hand.

To talk to Cortana;

Click on the Cortana icon located on the taskbar.

For effective communication and improved efficiency, speak clearly when talking to Cortana and ensure an active internet connection.

5.2.1 PERSONALIZING YOUR CORTANA SETTINGS

Go to Cortana > talk to Cortana

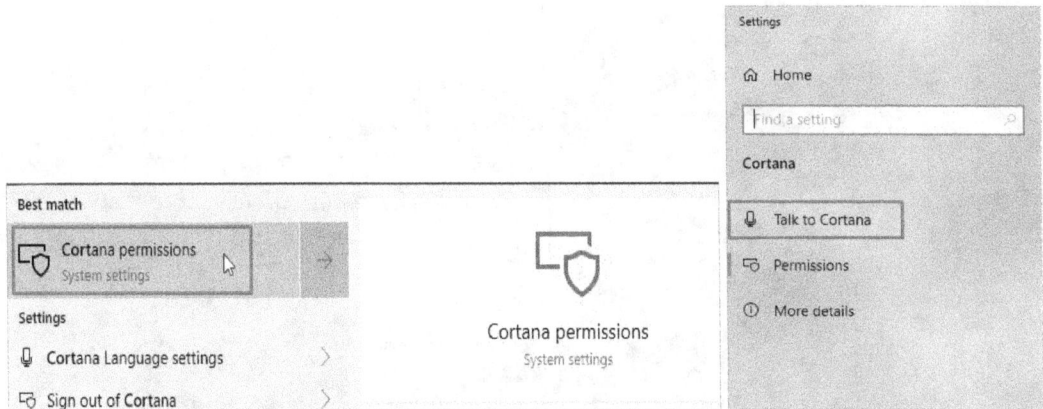

You can switch on or off the **'Hey Cortana'** toggle. Switching it on will let Cortana respond to you when you say 'hey Cortana' even when your computer is in sleeping mode.

However, the feature may affect your battery life because Cortana is always working hard and ready to be activated when she hears your voice.

➢ **USING THE KEYBOARD SHORTCUT**
1. From the Talk to Cortana option, scroll down to the **Keyboard shortcut.**
2. Switch on the toggle to activate the feature.

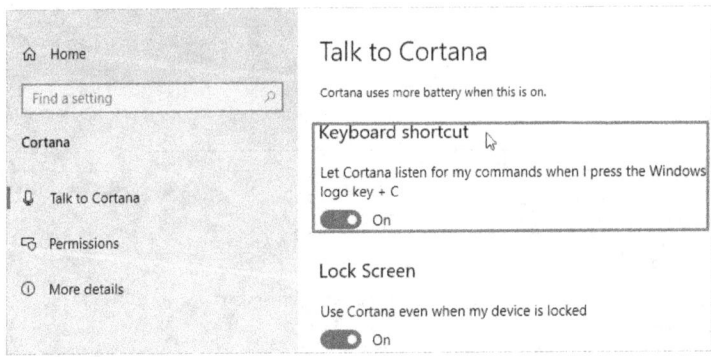

3. Press the Windows Key + D to go back to the desktop
4. Confirm the option by pressing Windows key + C.

Cortana can help perform and manage essential tasks. Some of the cool things that she can assist you with are;
- Setting alarm for you.
- Searching for almost anything on your computer and the web.
- Giving updates on weather conditions.
- Performing calculations and unit conversions.
- Sleeping your laptop or computer and lots more.

5.2.2 SETTING THE ALARM WITH CORTANA.

Assuming you have an important meeting scheduled for 12 pm, and you will like to get a reminder at exactly 11:45. You can quickly request Cortana to set an alarm for you. To do this;
1. Click on the Cortana icon already pinned to the taskbar or Press Windows Key + C if the feature is activated on your Cortana settings.

2. Click on the microphone icon to converse with Cortana.

3. Ask Cortana to remind you when it is 11:45 am

5.2.3 SEARCHING FOR INFORMATION ON YOUR COMPUTER

Imagine you have been working on an important task using Microsoft office word, and you wished to extract information from Microsoft Office Excel that has not been pinned to your taskbar. Then, you can quickly ask Cortana to open excel for you. Doing this will minimize the time required for scanning through your app list in the start menu or the time required to search in the search box.

To open your excel file with Cortana;
1. Click on the Cortana icon on your taskbar
2. Click on the microphone to talk to Cortana
3. Ask Cortana to open Excel.

5.2.4 SEARCHING INFORMATION ON THE WEB WITH CORTANA

One of the excellent features of Cortana is its ability to help the user search for any information on the internet. For example, assume that you are working on a project, which prompts you to check for the boiling point of water. You can quickly ask Cortana to search for this information.

1. Click on the Cortana icon on your Taskbar.
2. Then click on the microphone icon.
3. Ask Cortana for the boiling point of water.

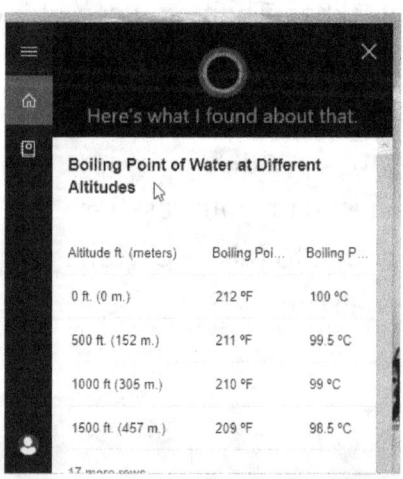

You can utilize the basic steps above to request the weather information of any location of your choice from Cortana.

5.2.5 PERFORMING CALCULATIONS WITH CORTANA

What if you are carrying out engineering calculations and are provided with a value in System International Unit? You must convert to Field or American unit to get a consistent result. Provided in one of your calculations, you want Cortana to convert 20 kilograms (Kg) to Pounds(lb.).

1. Click on the Cortana icon in the taskbar
2. Click on the Microphone icon
3. Ask Cortana to convert 20 kilograms to Pounds

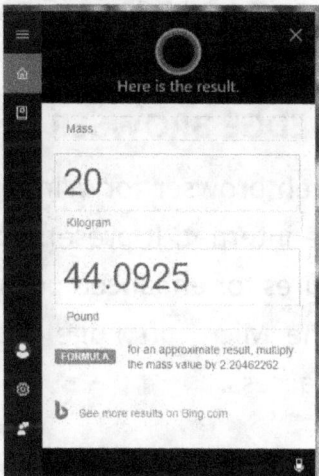

5.2.6 SHUTTING DOWN YOUR LAPTOP WITH CORTANA

After completing all the planned tasks on your computer, you may wish to shut it down. You can easily do this with Cortana's help.

1. Click Windows key + C if activated in the settings, or click on the Cortana icon on the taskbar.
2. Click on the Microphone icon
3. Ask Cortana to Shut down your computer or Laptop.

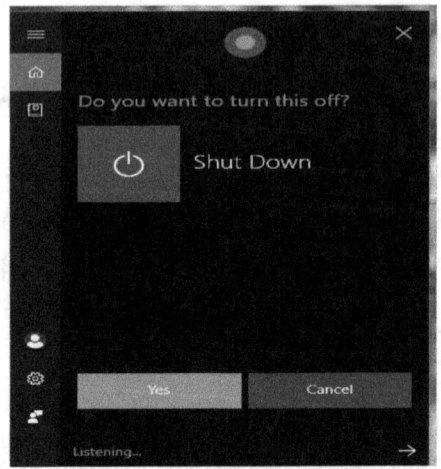

Cortana will ask you if you want to shut down. Click **Yes** to confirm.

You can follow the above steps if you wish to sleep or restart your computer.

5.3 USING MICROSOFT EDGE BROWSER

Microsoft Edge, a built-in web browser for Windows 10, is one of the best web browsers available to surf the internet. It presents an improvement over internet explorer and has several features for enhanced productivity. Some of the immense benefits of browsing with the Microsoft Edge browser are minimum usage of power, safe and fast internet access.

To open the edge browser;

Go to Start > Microsoft Edge

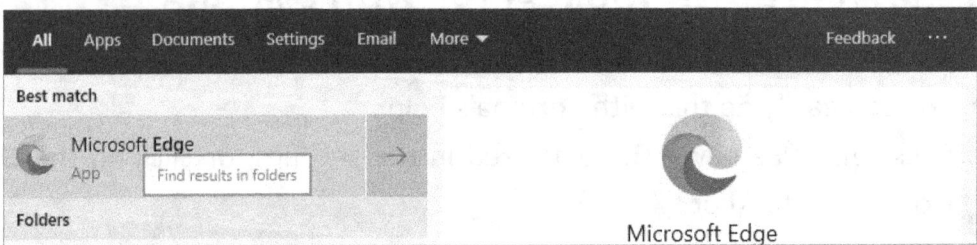

5.3.1 FEATURES OF MICROSOFT EDGE BROWSER

Some unique features of Microsoft Edge are highlighted below;
- ➢ **READ ALOUD**

The read-aloud feature utilizes different voice options to assist the reader in reading out the text or contents of both web pages and e-books. This feature is frequently updated to improve its performance.

To use the read-aloud feature;
1. Click on the three dots located at the top right corner beside the address bar.

2. Select **Read Aloud**

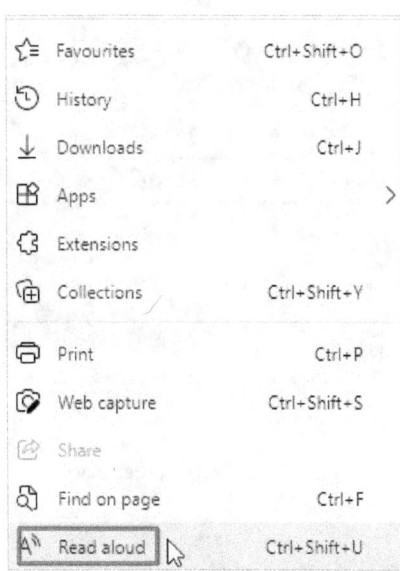

Alternatively, you can press Ctrl + Shift + U on your keyboard to directly access Read-aloud.

To customize the voice for your Read aloud;
1. Click on Voice options

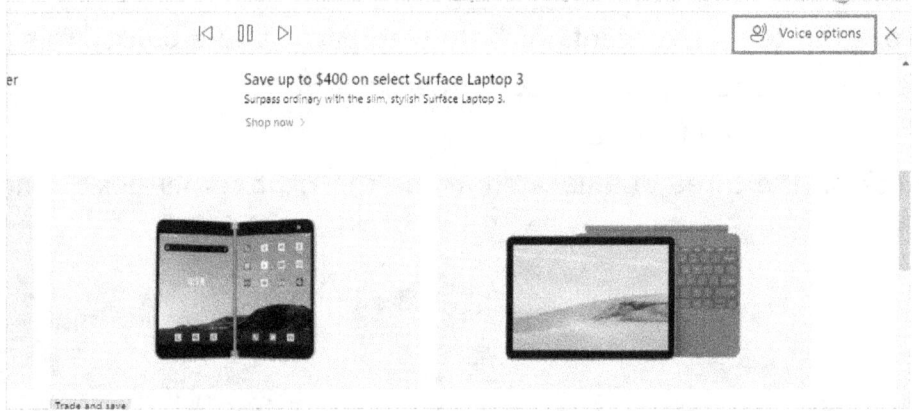

2. Select your preferred from the list of voices in the **Choose a voice** drop-down menu.

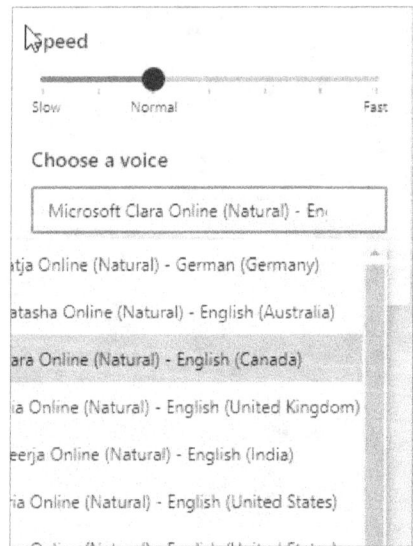

You can adjust the speed in the space provided.

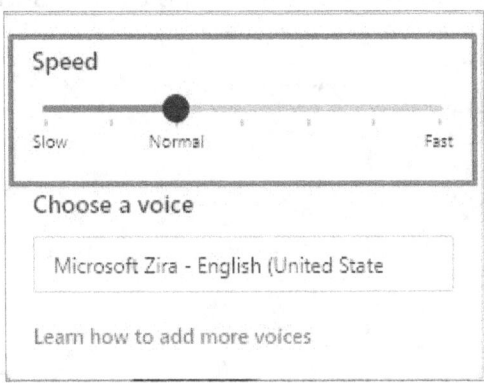

➢ READING VIEW

The immersive reader tool in Microsoft Edge helps you stay focused and read without displaying ads. While using reading view or immersive reader, you can use different features such as Read aloud, adjusting the font size, and customizing the background themes. In addition, you can print this page directly without any ads. However, the reading view does not work for all web pages. If a webpage supports the reading view, you will see the immersive reader icon added to the address bar of the Edge browser.

3. Click on the reading view or immersive reader icon in the address bar to access the reading view.

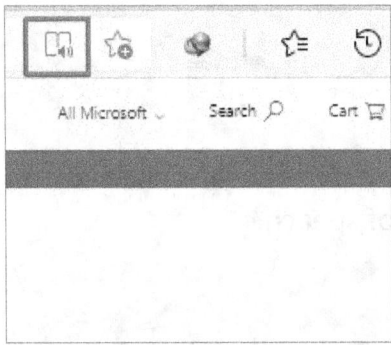

While on the reading view mode, Read Aloud, text preferences, Grammar tools, and Reading preferences should appear just below the address bar.

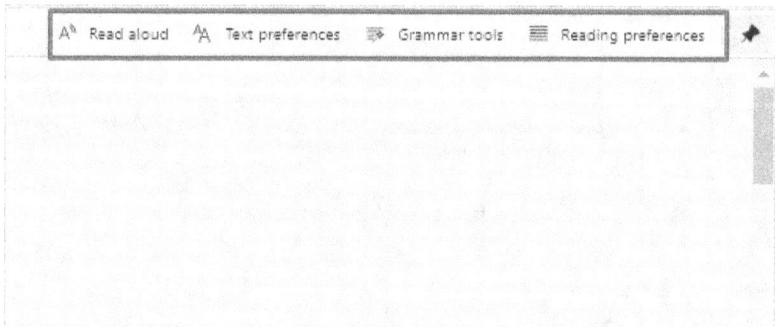

Reading preferences has a line focus to help concentrate more while in the reading mode and the translate option available to translate the entire page.

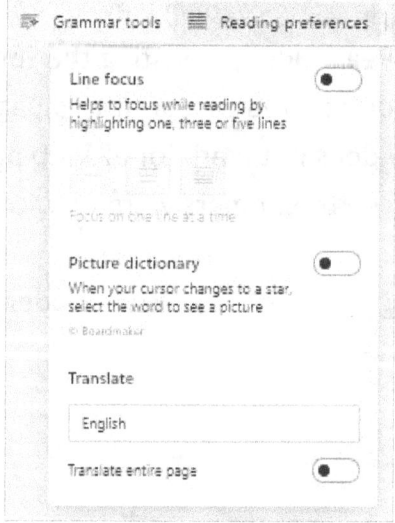

Grammar Tools: The grammar tool can split texts on the webpage into syllables, and their respective parts of speech.

Text Preferences: Text preferences help you to customize text sizes while in reading mode. There is a text space feature that lets you space the texts to make them easier to read. Page themes option helps you change the background color, making the display background match your preference.

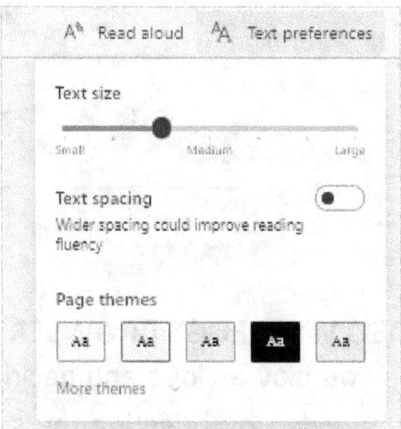

> **PINNING YOUR PREFERRED WEBSITE PAGE TO THE TASKBAR**

It's very likely that you have preferred or frequently visited websites. To ease the stress of opening your browser and visiting the website every time, you can pin the website pages on your taskbar with Edge browser. To pin any web page;

1. Click the three dots located at the top right corner of the browser
2. Go to **more tools** and select pin to taskbar.

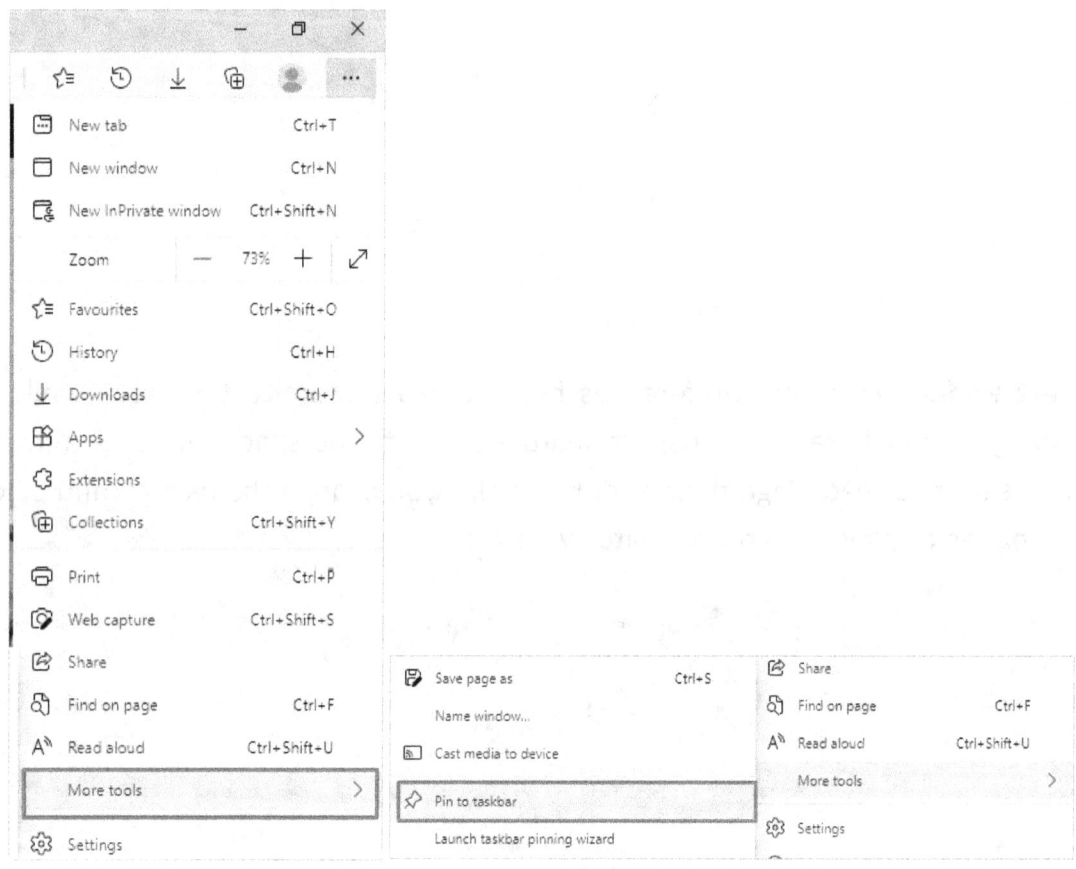

> **MUTING YOUR VIDEO WITH EDGE BROWSER**

There are instances when you play a video and decide to open another tab. You can mute the already played video by selecting the speaker icon in the previous tab.

5.4   USING THE WINDOWS 10 CALCULATOR

Windows calculator app has some advanced features different from previous versions of windows calculators. The new design has made it possible for users to convert from one unit to another, thereby making calculations easier. It can also help us to convert from one currency to another quickly.

To access the calculator app;

Go to Start > Calculator.

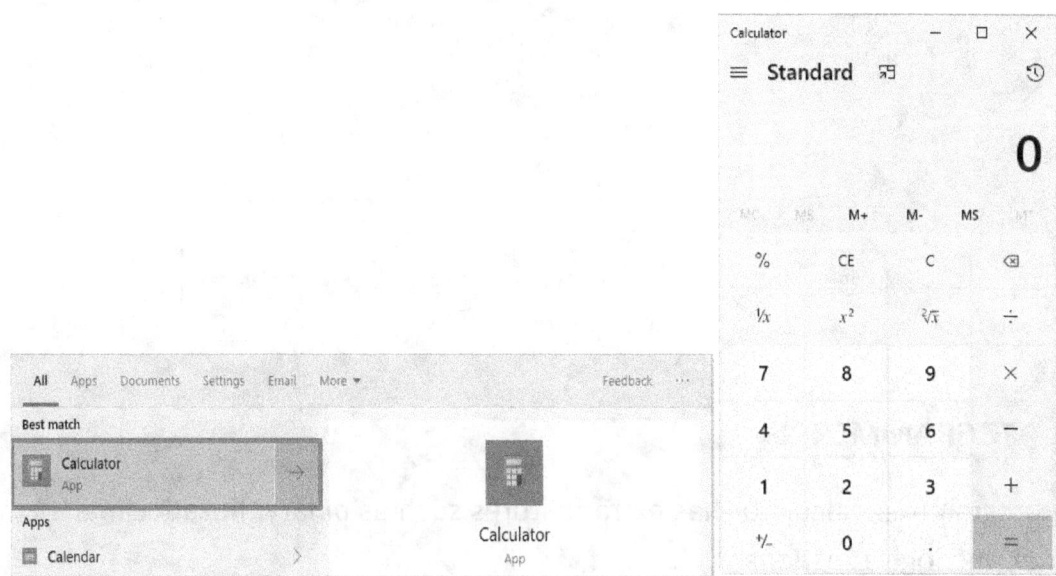

By default, the standard calculator, similar to the conventional calculator, is displayed. You can use other options within the application by clicking on the three dash (≡) lines at the top left corner of the calculator display.

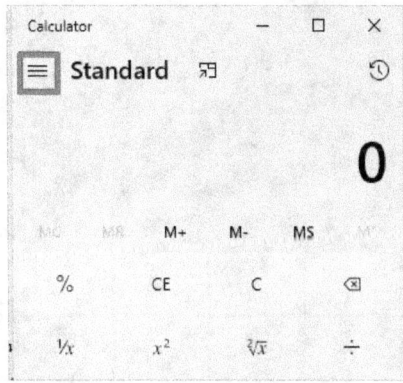

➢ **SCIENTIFIC CALCULATOR**

The scientific calculator resembles well known scientific calculator, with added features like trigonometric and logarithmic function.

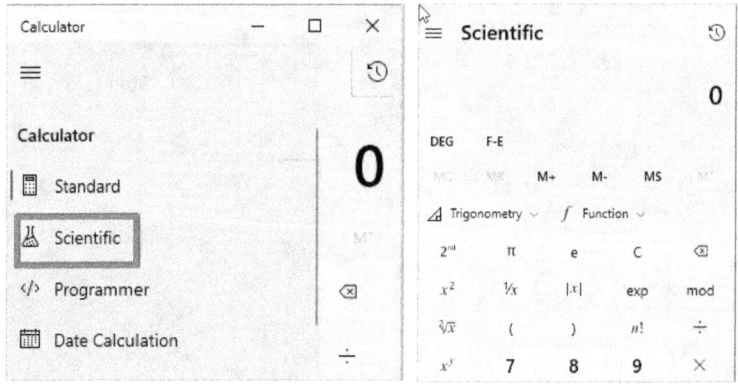

➢ **PROGRAMMER**

The programmer calculator has extra features such as binary, hexadecimal, octa-decimal, and logic functions.

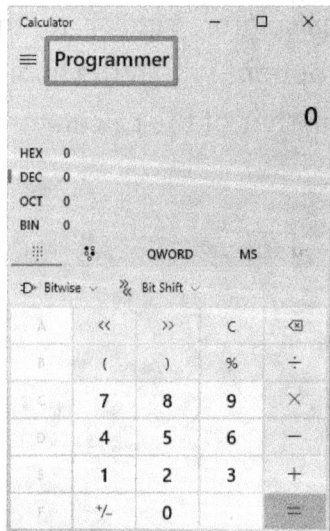

5.4.1 DATE CALCULATION

You can use the date calculations to either add or subtract or find the difference between dates.

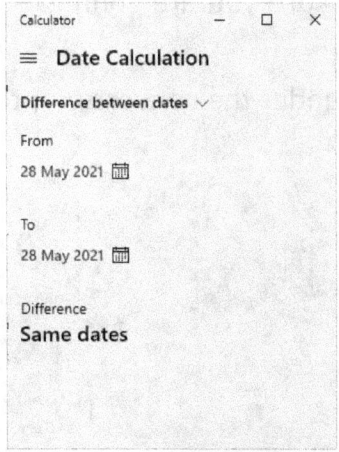

5.4.2 CONVERTER

The converter option in the Windows 10 calculator app is divided into different options; Currency, Volume and Length, Energy, Temperature, Speed, Area, Time, Power, data, Pressure, and Pressure.

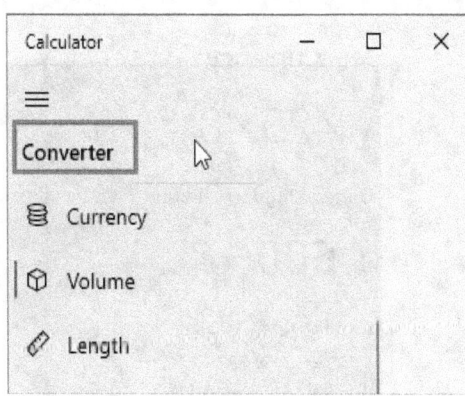

➢ **CURRENCY CONVERTER**

The currency converter makes it possible to convert from one currency to another currency of your choice. For instance, you may wish to convert 600 us dollars to UK pounds. Make sure you are connected to the internet and take the following steps;

4. Click on the currency under the converter option in the calculator app.

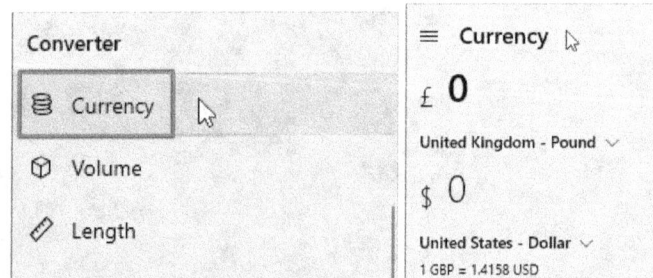

5. Select **United States – Dollar** from either of the two drop-down menus and enter 600
6. Choose **United Kingdom - Pound** from the options in the second drop-down menu. You will see that the 600 US Dollar converts to the corresponding value in UK Pounds.

➢ VOLUME CONVERTER

Volume converter helps with the volumetric conversion from one unit to another.
1. Under converter, Click on the volume option.

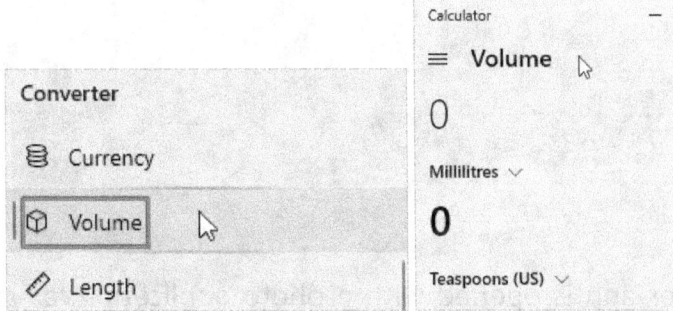

2. Select the unit from any of the drop-down and enter the known value.
3. Choose the desired unit from the second drop-down to get the unknown value.

You can use the explanations above for other conversions, such as converting Kilograms to pounds (lbs.) or metric tons, Fahrenheit to degree Celsius or Kelvin, kg per hour to meter per seconds, and lots more.

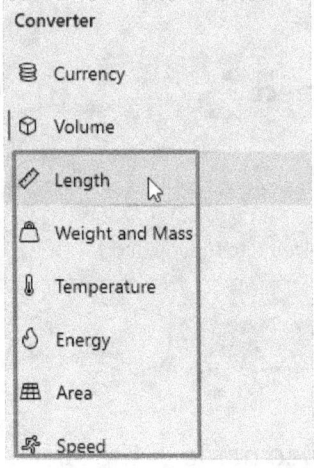

5.5 USING THE VIDEO EDITOR

Windows 10 has a built-in video editor. To access this editor;
1. Go to Start > Video editor

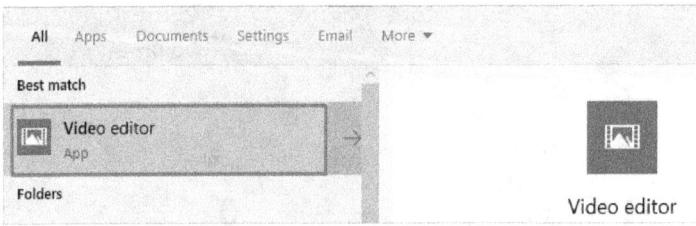

The video editor app is opened with a photo application, as seen on the video editor page.

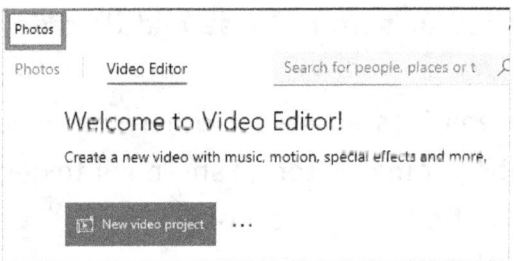

To start editing your videos;
1. Click on **New video project**

2. Type your preferred video name in the space provided.

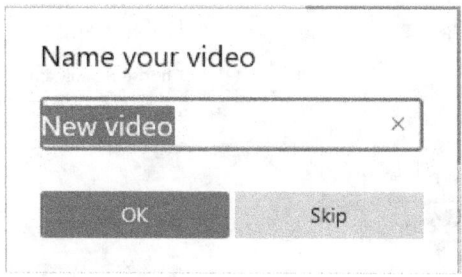

3. Click **OK**

A new page showing the project library and the storyboard will be displayed. You can add different videos and photos to your project library and drag your files to the storyboard to make your video. You can utilize the **Add title card icon**, **Text, motion**, and **filter tools** to edit your videos. You can also preview as you work on your video.

5.6 CHANGING WINDOWS DEFAULT APPS

Some applications such as edge browser and photo viewer are set by default in Windows 10. However, you can change these apps if you wish to use one of your installed applications for the same purpose. To change your default apps;

1. Go to Start > Settings.
2. Click on Apps to access **Apps and features** settings.

3. Select **Default apps**

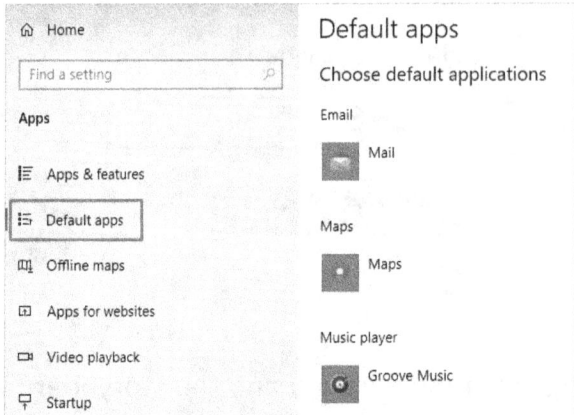

4. Click on the default application that you want to change.
5. Select the new application that you want to use from the **Choose an application** page.

You can reset the changes made to your default apps by clicking the Reset button.

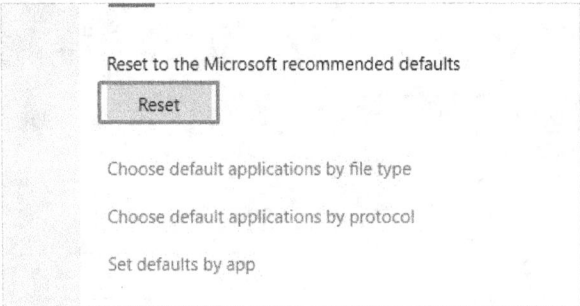

5.7 UNINSTALLING APPLICATIONS

You can uninstall any application on your Windows 10 operating system using two different methods;

5.7.1 SHORTCUT METHOD

The shortcut method is the fastest way to uninstall your applications. To uninstall using the shortcut method;

1. Click the start button or press the Windows key on your keyboard to access the start menu.
2. From the application list, scroll down to look for the exact application to be uninstalled.
3. Right-click on the application and then select **Uninstall**.

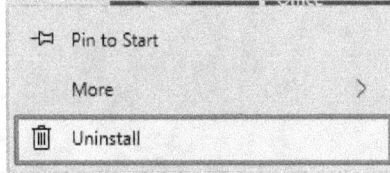

5.7.2 UNINSTALLING FROM THE CONTROL PANEL

You can also uninstall your preferred application from the control panel.
1. Go to start > Control panel > Program and features

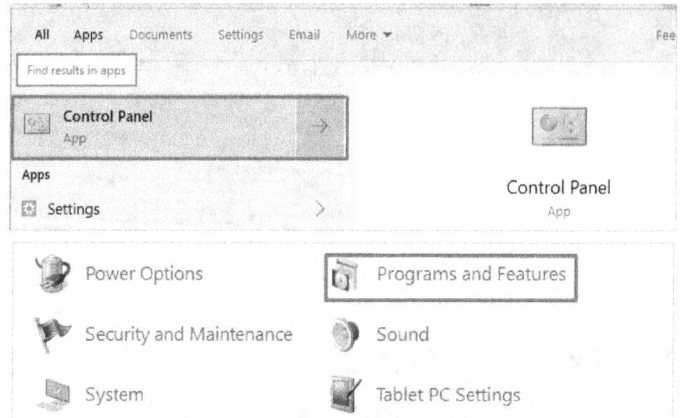

2. From the program option, click **Uninstall a program.**

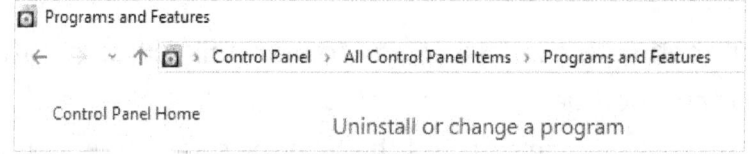

3. Double click on the program to be uninstalled

SECTION SIX - WINDOWS FILE EXPLORER

The windows file explorer provides you with an opportunity to easily manage your files and folders. You can customize how these folders are arranged and displayed on your computer.

To access the file explorer from your device;

1. Click on File Explorer icon on the taskbar or Press Windows key + E to access the windows file explorer.

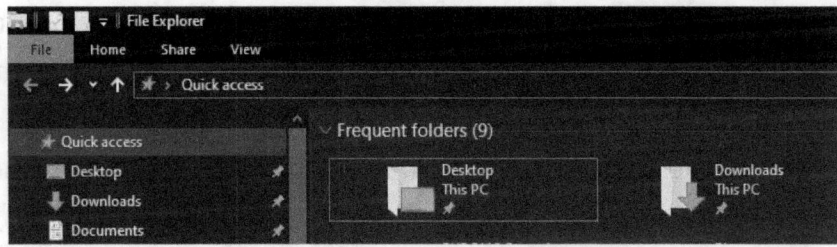

2. Click on **This PC** from the Quick access on the left side of your computer screen.

This area is divided into two major parts: '**Folders'** and '**Devices and drives**.

> Folders (7)
> Devices and drives (3)

The folders area consists of the main folders where you access most of your files. The folder is classified into Desktop, Downloads, Documents, Pictures, Music, and Videos.

However, the '**Devices and drives**' section shows the storage area (C for windows and D for recovery) and any device connected to the computer, such as mobile phones and external hard drives.

By clicking any of the folders in the **Folder** section of This PC, you should notice that the top left corner has four major categories or tabs: the **home tab**, **the share, and the view tab.**

6.1 HOME TAB

If you click on the Home tab in the menu bar, you will see that it has different options that you can utilize to ease your work. Some of these options are **copy** and **paste.** If you choose to copy any document from the selected folder, use the **copy** option to copy the document and then paste it anywhere on your computer. On the other hand, if a document is copied from elsewhere, such as the desktop area, you can paste it on your selected folder in the file explorer by clicking on the paste option. You can also use the **cut** option to cut any file and move elsewhere. The **home tab** has options for creating a folder and also for deleting and renaming documents.

6.2 SHARE TAB

The windows share tab is a useful tool for sharing files or documents with people. You can control who you share your files with and how they are shared. To share your document;

1. Select the document or file that you want to share
2. Click the **share tab** located in the upper left corner of your screen.

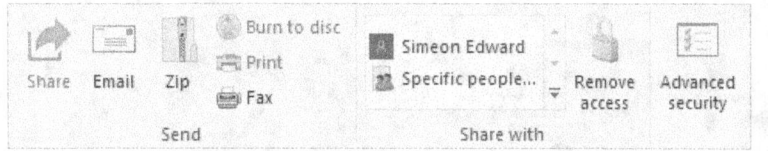

3. Click on the **share icon** and select the application you want to use for sharing the file or document.

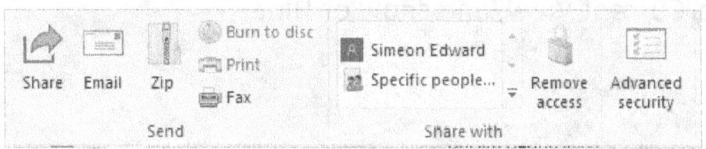

You can use the email option if you have it configured on your computer.

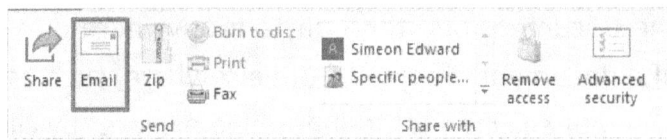

You can also share multiple files by holding the control key on your keyboard and selecting the files you would like to share.

To compress your documents before sharing;
1. Select the file that needs to be compressed
2. Click on the **Share tab**
3. Click on the **zip** button to compress the file or document.

6.3   VIEW TAB.

From the word View, this option lets you customize your layout in the file explorer.

The view tab is divided into;
Panes, Layout, Current View, and show or Hide.

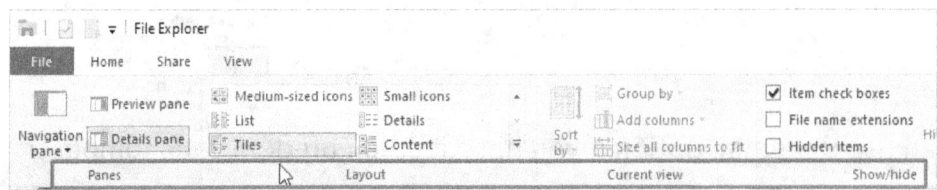

Panes: The panes section of the view tab consists of the Navigation pane, Preview pane, and details pane

The preview pane is suitable for e-books, office documents, and files such as pictures. This tool lets you see the contents of the selected document or file.

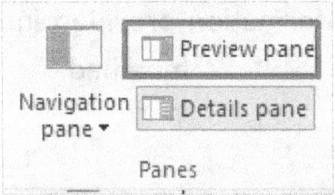

Details pane, on the other hand, cannot be used for previewing the selected file. It does give all the necessary information about the document.

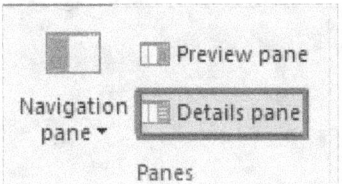

Layout Section

The layout section of the View tab allows the users to have full control of how their files are viewed and arranged within the file explorer. It consists of extra-large, large, medium, and small-sized icons. There are also options for lists, details, contents, and tiles in the layout section.

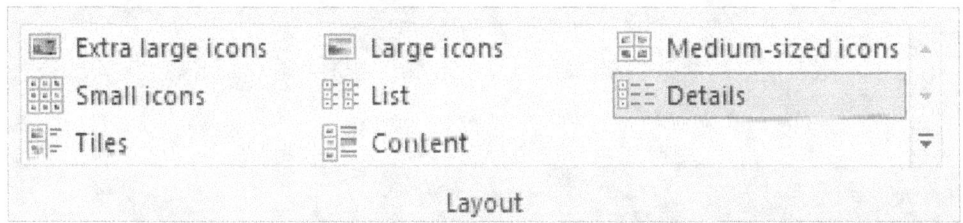

While using the **List view**, you can scroll to the left side of the screen. It presents an option for you if you have a large number of files and want to view them all at once or quickly search for information.

If you have chosen to use the content view option, you will have the opportunity to see the information of the files or documents within the selected folder in the file explorer. Some of the information provided include dimension and type (for pictures), date modified and more.

SECTION SEVEN - MANAGING DEVICE CONNECTIONS

It is possible to connect your computer to a wide range of devices and drives. Think of a situation when you have a picture on your phone that you intend to use as the background image on your computer or an important document to be transferred from your pen drive to your computer. Also, you may want to back up your files from your laptop to an external hard drive or want to print an important document directly from your computer. The instances given above are typical representations of direct or wired connections to your device.

Apart from wired or direct connections, you can also make wireless connections such as Bluetooth and Wi-Fi connections.

7.1 BLUETOOTH CONNECTIONS

Connecting to any device via Bluetooth is easy on windows 10. All you need to do is to enable Bluetooth on your device. To make Bluetooth connections;

Go to Action center or press Windows logo key + A

Click on the Bluetooth icon to enable it.

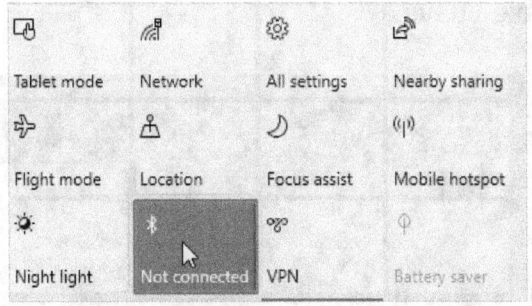

To connect to a Bluetooth enabled device;
1. Right-click on the Bluetooth icon in the Action center and click **Go to settings.**

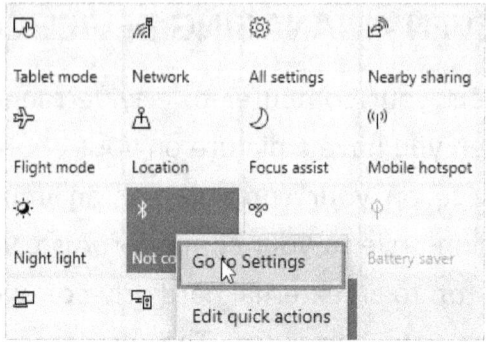

2. Click on **'Add Bluetooth or other device'**

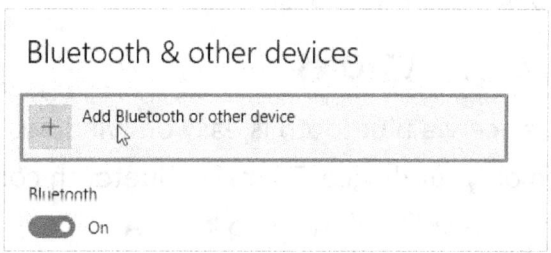

3. On the 'Add a device page', click the **Bluetooth** option to connect to a Bluetooth enabled device

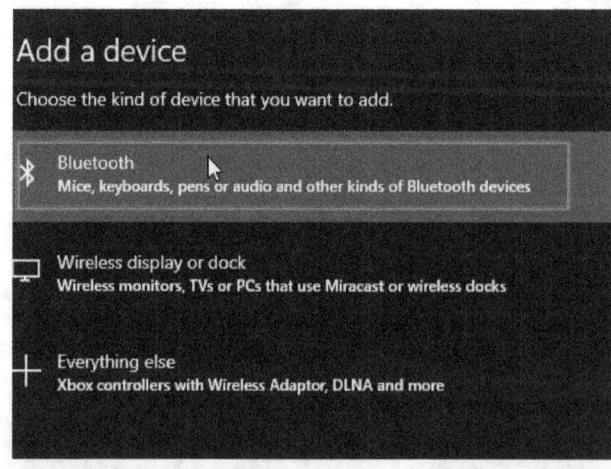

7.2 CONNECTING TO A PEN DRIVE

When you connect a pen drive or any form of external drive to your device, it should be automatically detected by your computer. To access the information on the drive;
1. Go to File Explorer
2. Click on **This PC**.

The drive should be displayed on **the 'Devices and drive'** section of This PC.

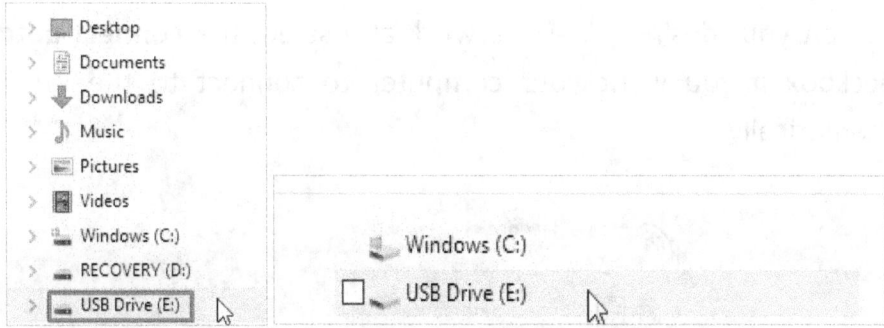

To eject a plugged external drive from your computer;
4. Click on the small up arrow button in the taskbar's notification area and click on the USB drive icon.

7.3 WI-FI CONNECTIONS

Making Wi-Fi connections on windows 10 is an easy task that requires few steps. You must ensure that your Wi-Fi in the action center is activated to detect the available network automatically.

1. Click on the network connections icon in the notification area of the taskbar.

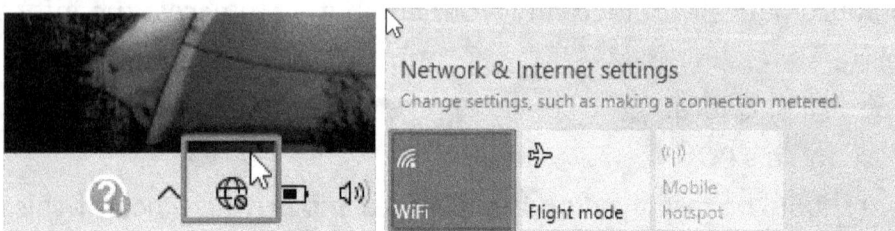

2. Click on your desired Wi-Fi network and select the **connect automatically** checkbox if you want your computer to connect to the Wi-Fi network automatically.

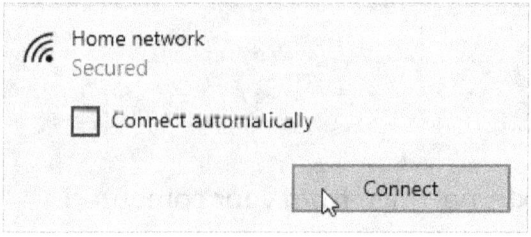

3. Click on **Connect**

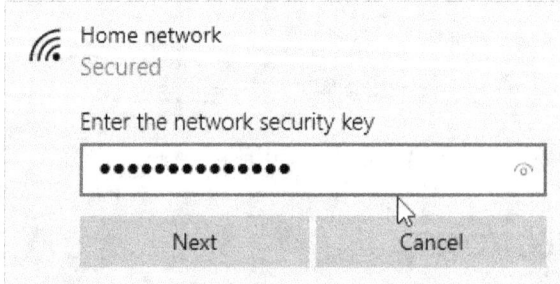

4. Enter the Wi-Fi password if you are connecting for the first time or if the password has been changed.

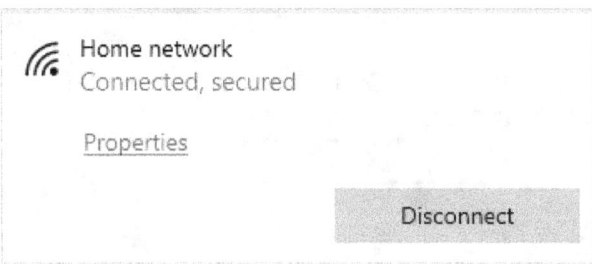

7.4 USING THE MIRACAST

Let us assume that you have an interesting movie saved on your computer which you want your family to see. You can cast your device screen on a bigger screen, such as your Smart TV. To achieve this, you need to ensure that your smart TV support screencast.

1. Go to Start > Settings > Devices
2. Click on **Bluetooth and other devices**

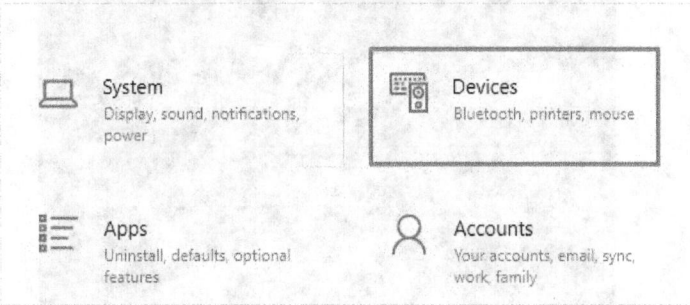

3. Click the plus (+) sign indicating **'Add Bluetooth or other device'**.

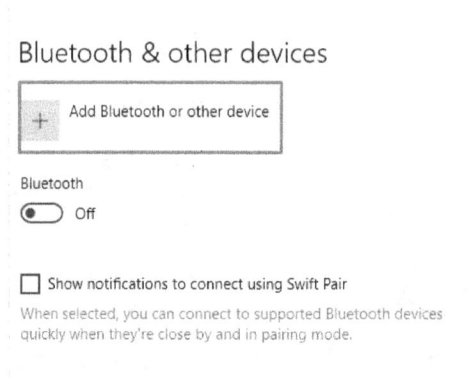

With TV's Miracast turned on, select the **'Wireless display or dock'** option to detect and connect to the other device (your TV).

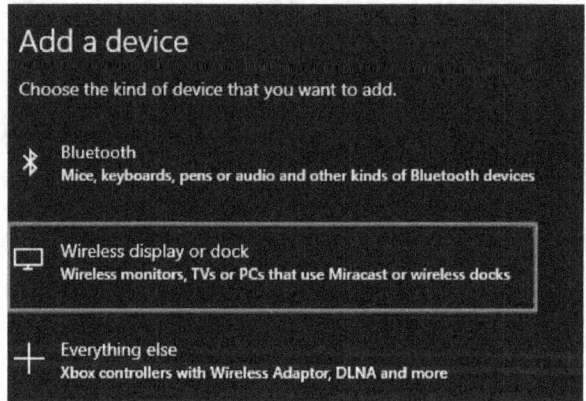

7.5 CONNECTING TO PRINTER

1. Go to Device > Printer and scanners.
2. Click on **'Add printers & scanners'** to add a new printer.

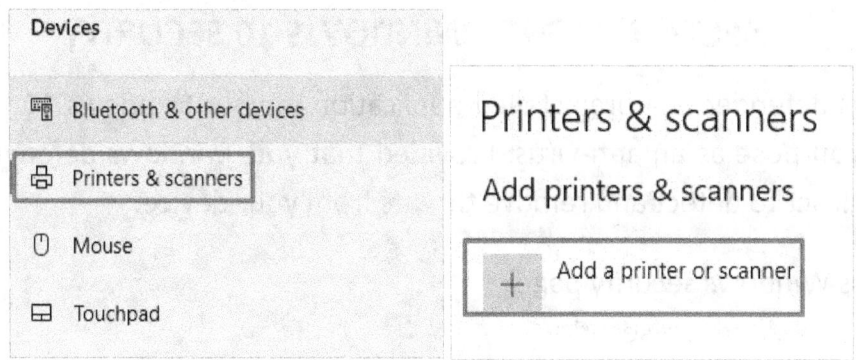

Windows will select the last printer you used as the default printer. You can change this setting by clicking the '**Allow Windows to manage my default printer'** checkbox.

SECTION EIGHT - WINDOWS 10 SECURITY

Windows defender is a preinstalled application in your Windows 10 that serves the same purpose as an anti-virus. Provided that your windows defender is up to date, it will act to detect and remove threats from your device.

To access Windows security page;
Go to Start > Windows security

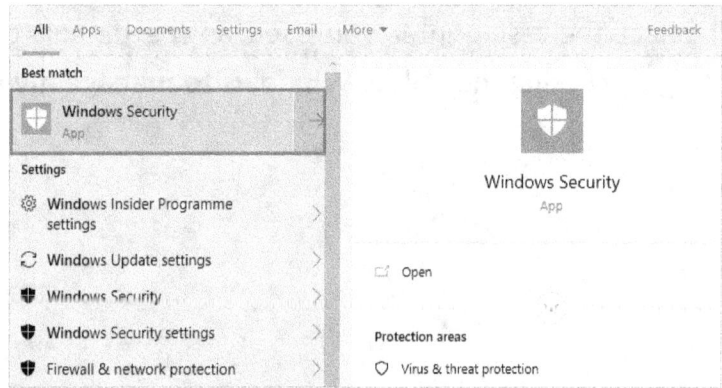

Clicking on the **windows security** will take you to the Windows security home page showing security at a glance. It shows all the security options available on your device. If the features shown here are marked green, there is no required action to be taken. Yellow and red checks indicate a need to fix something to make the application work properly.

Windows 10 security is divided into the following categories;

8.1 VIRUS AND THREAT PROTECTION

Virus and Threat protection is an important window security feature that helps you scan and identify threats on your computer.

Click on the '**Virus & threat protection** icon in the windows security home or Click on the icon on the left side to access the Virus and threat protection page.

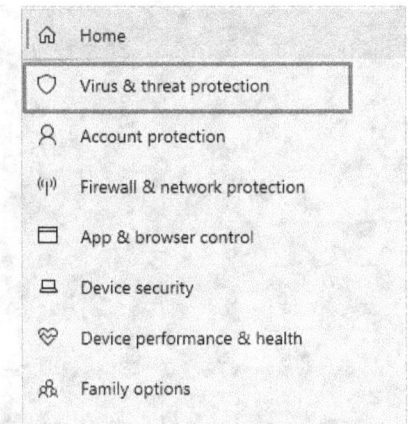

8.1.1 CURRENT THREATS

The first option available to you on the virus and threat protection page is the current threats. It is known as a current threat because it identifies current threats within your computer. This feature can help you start a new scan, give the history of previous scans executed, and help to identify the threats that have been allowed by the user. You can run a quick scan by clicking on the Quick scan button in the Current threat area.

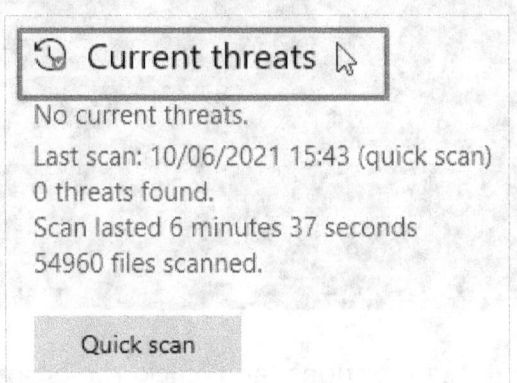

To personalize your scan, click on **the Scan options** link.

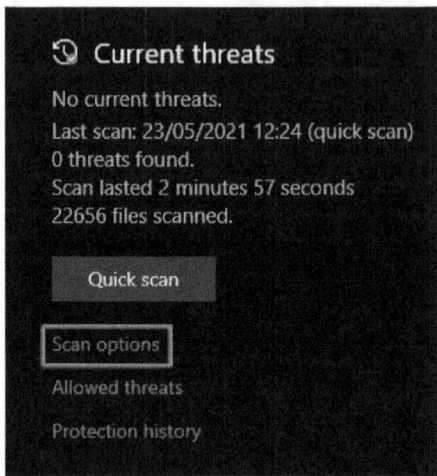

The scan options page provides you with four different options, which are; Quick scan, Full scan, Custom scan, and Windows Defender Offline scan.

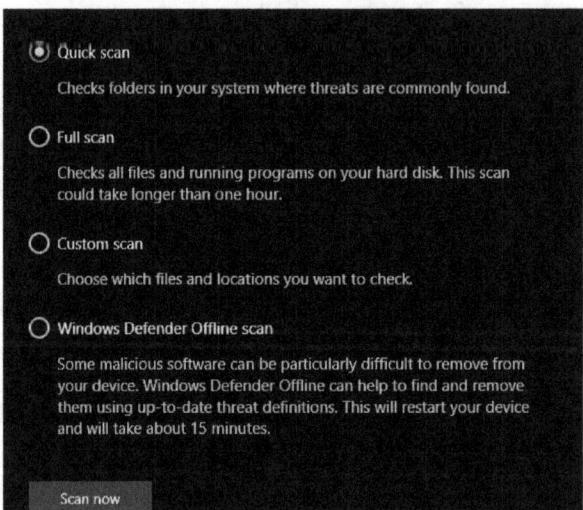

Select your preferred scan options and click the **scan now** button to start scanning for threats on your computer.

You can click the **Allowed threats** link to see the threats you have allowed to run on your computer. You can also make use of the **protection history** link.

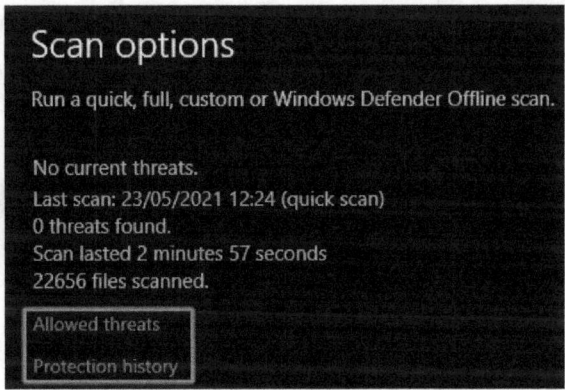

8.1.2 VIRUS & THREAT PROTECTION SETTINGS

You can customize this setting by clicking the manage settings link.

Real-time protection helps to stop the installation of malware on your device. If turned off for any reason, it will automatically be turned on after a while.

Other available options are;

Cloud-delivered protection, Automatic sample submission, and tamper protection.

You can manage controlled folder access, exclude some items from being scanned and customize your notification settings using the provided link.

8.2 ACCOUNT PROTECTION

The account protection option helps to secure the user's account. To explore the available options, click on the **Account protection** icon or use the icon on the left side of the screen.

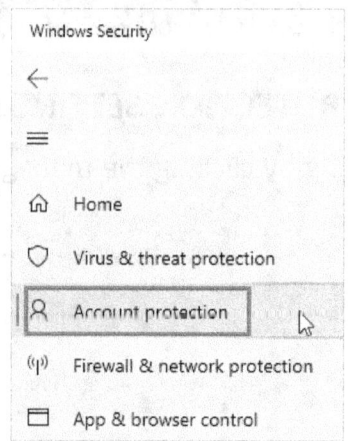

8.3 FIREWALL & NETWORK PROTECTION

A Firewall is an important tool that helps users gain full control of their private information by blocking outsiders' unauthorized access to their network.

Firewall & network protection is classified into three major categories:

- **Domain network:** Also known as workplace network
- **The Private or discoverable network** is your home network that friends or family can access.
- **A public network,** known as a non-discoverable network, is hidden due to the likelihood of the network been accessed by strangers.

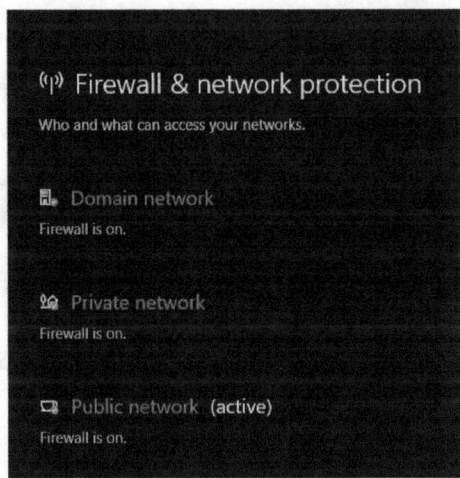

The **firewall & network protection** setting protects your device when accessing any of the three networks mentioned above.

8.3.1 ALLOWING AN APPLICATION THROUGH THE FIREWALL

You may choose to allow a particular app through the firewall & network protection by clicking on **Allow an app through the firewall** link.

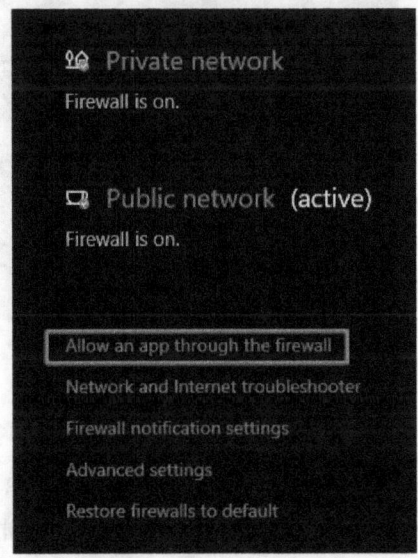

8.3.2 NETWORK AND INTERNET TROUBLESHOOTER

If you have difficulties using the internet or connecting to your network, you may use this link to trouble and fix the problem.

8.3.3 FIREWALL NOTIFICATION SETTINGS

You can customize the firewall notification such that it informs you when it detects and blocks network threats.

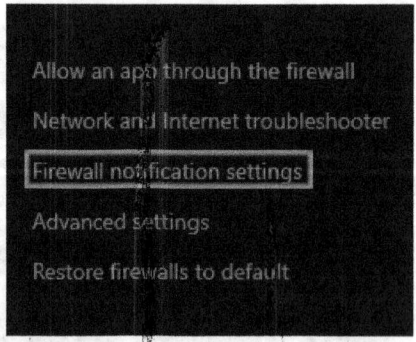

8.3.4 ADVANCED SETTINGS

The advanced setting is utilized if you are very good at making changes to the firewall. It allows you to make changes. However, using advanced firewall settings is not recommended as it can make the system more vulnerable.

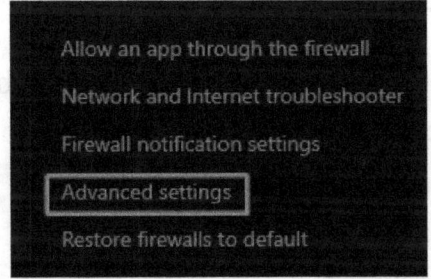

8.3.5 RESTORE FIREWALLS TO DEFAULT

This feature helps you restore firewalls to the default setting if you observe an issue with the way it functions.

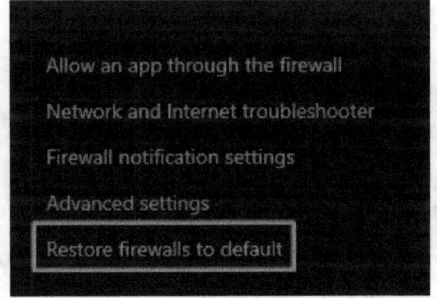

8.4 APPS & BROWSER CONTROL

The Microsoft SmartScreen requires the settings to protect the user from malicious applications, downloads, and websites.

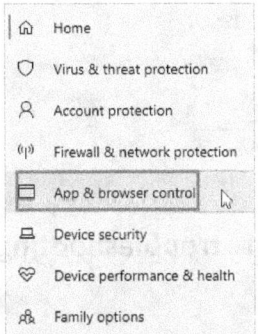

8.5 DEVICE SECURITY

The device security is also known as the computer's built-in security tool. From the windows security, click on **the Device security** link to access the device security page.

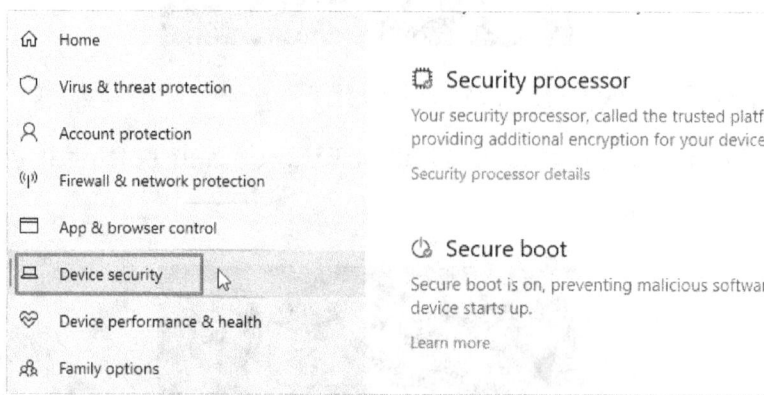

8.5.1 SECURITY PROCESSOR

Security processor provides additional encryption for your device. There may be instances when this security feature will fail to operate properly. To check and fix this issue;

1. Click on the **Security processor details** link.

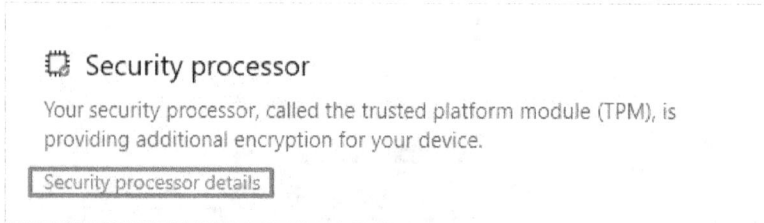

2. Click **security processor troubleshooting** to troubleshoot and fix the Security processor issue.

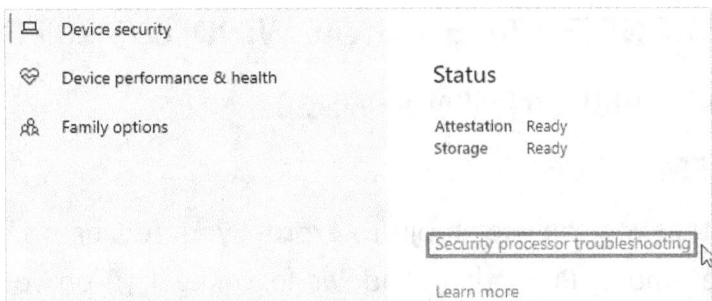

8.5.2 SECURE BOOT

The secure boot option prevents the loading of Rootkit, a dangerous Malware type when you start your computer. If the secure boot is not in place, this malware may hide and transfer user information.

8.6 DEVICE PERFORMANCE & HEALTH

This tool reports the computer's health and performance.

The health report is classified into Storage capacity, battery life, apps and software, and Windows time service.

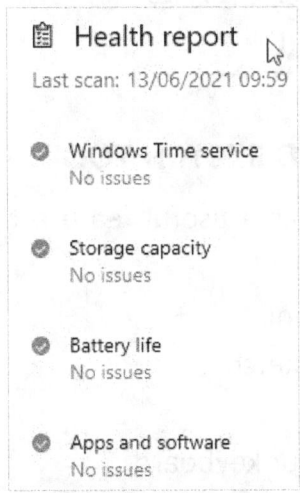

SECTION NINE – ADDITIONAL WINDOWS 10 FEATURES

9.1 TIPS AND TRICKS IN WINDOWS 10

9.1.1 USING EMOJIS

Do you know that you can use emojis to express your feelings in Windows 10?

To call up the emojis, Press the Windows logo key + (;) on your keyboard and select the best emojis that suit your feelings or expressions.

9.1.2 USING THE SNIP AND SKETCH TOOL

This Microsoft application has a useful feature that can capture any portion of your computer screen.

To use the snip and sketch tool;

1. Go to start > Snip and sketch

Alternatively;

Press Windows key + S on your keyboard.

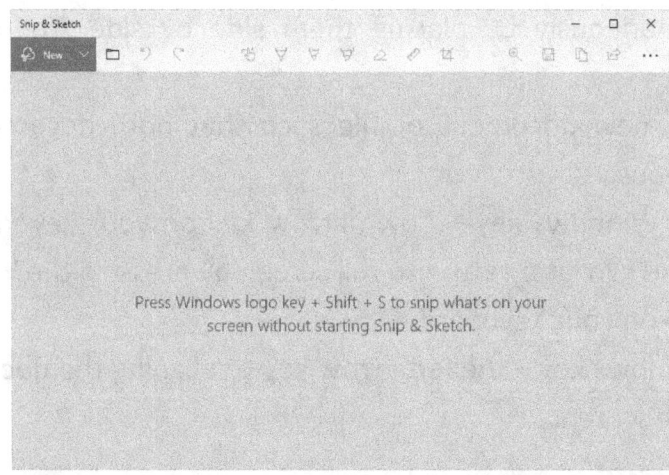

2. Click on **new** to start snipping.

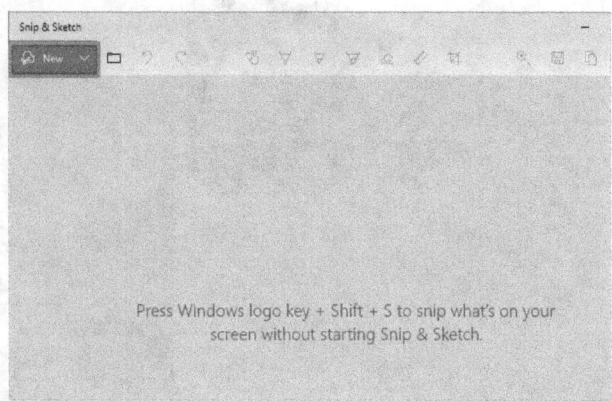

3. Crop out the portion of the page you wish to capture.

You can make further changes and edit with the available tools.

9.1.3 WINDOWS SNAPPING

As a user, you can work on multiple files simultaneously on your desktop. You can position the files without manually dragging or moving them into position.

Assuming you have been typing on Microsoft office word and suddenly recall information that needs to be pulled out of another document. You can work on

both files simultaneously by placing them side by side. To use the windows snapping;
1. Open the new document or file such that both documents are opened simultaneously.
2. Press the Windows key + down arrow key on your keyboard to exit a full screen. You can later return to full screen by pressing the Windows key + Up arrow key on your keyboard.
3. Press Windows key + the left arrow key to aligning the document to the left side of the screen.

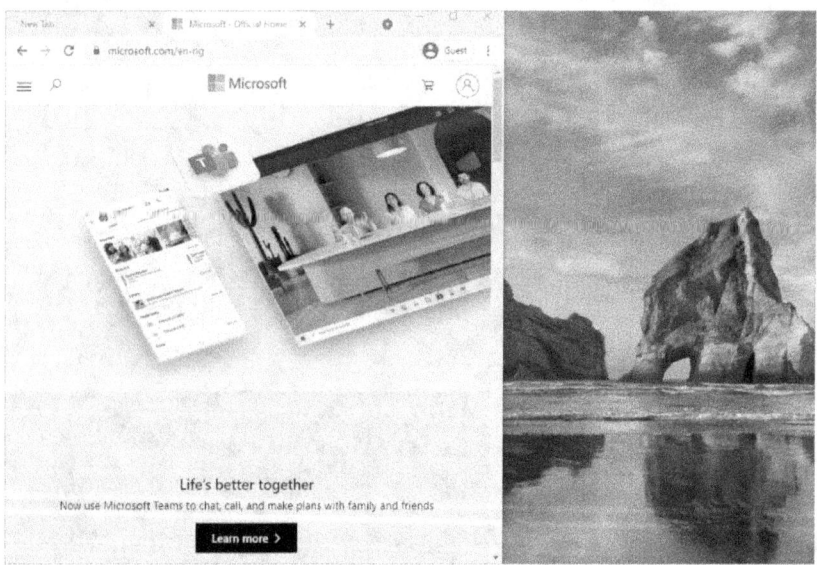

4. Press 'Windows key + the right arrow key' to aligning the file to the right side of the screen.

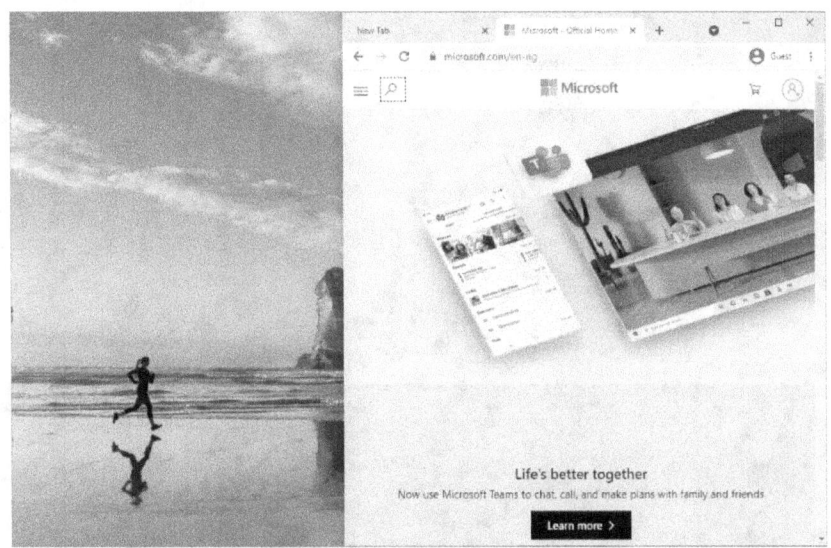

There are some personalization options available in the taskbar.

Right-click on the taskbar and select **cascade windows** to put one file on top of another.

Click on **'show windows stacked'** to position one file directly on top of another.

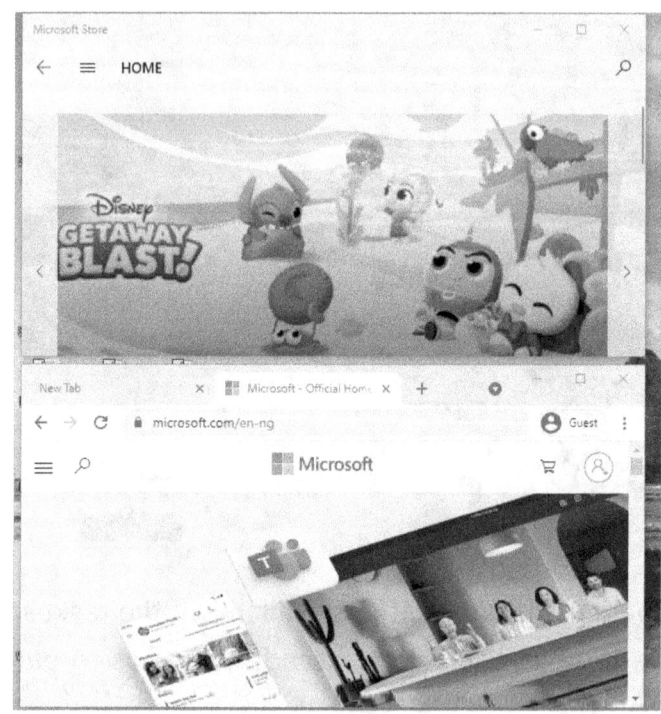

9.1.4 CUSTOMIZING YOUR WINDOWS UPDATE

Go to Start > Windows updates.

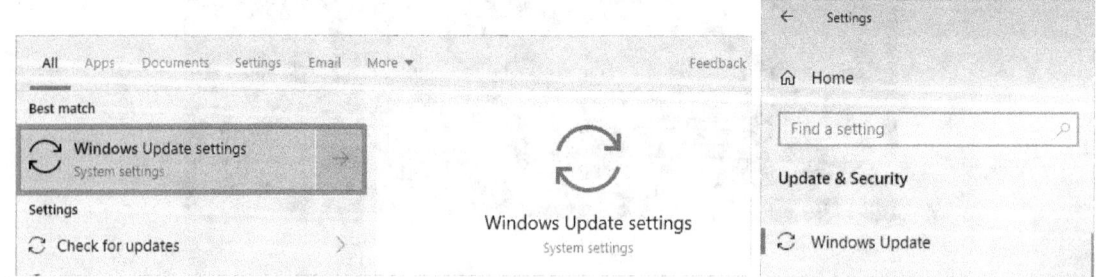

You can click the **'check for update'** button to scan for available updates.

You can also pause the updates for seven days or use the advanced options to customize further the period needed to pause your updates.

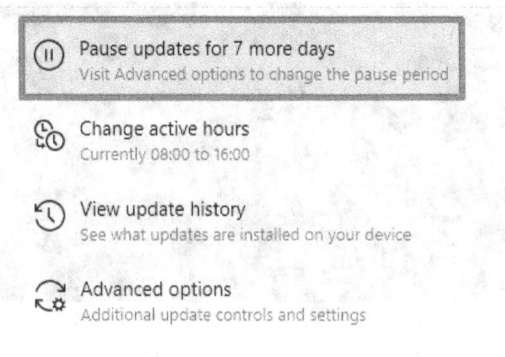

The **'View update history'** gives you information about the windows update that has been installed on your computer.

9.1.5 USING THE XBOX GAME BAR FOR SCREEN CAPTURE

1. Type game bar into the search box or press Windows key + G

2. Click on the capture icon or widget menu to access the capture menu.

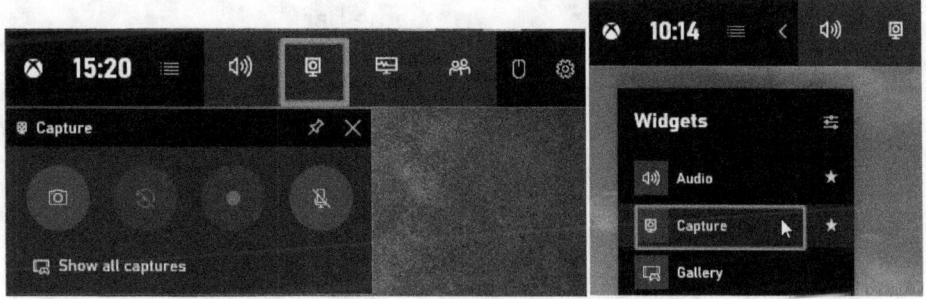

Click on the **take a screenshot** icon to capture the entire screen.

Click on the **start recording** icon or press the Windows key + Alt + R from your keyboard to record your screen.

To personalize the game bar settings;
Go to start > Game bar shortcuts

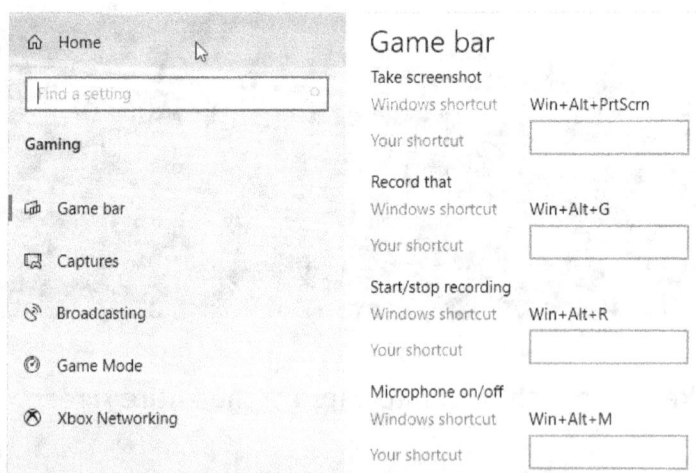

You can select the available options in the gaming area to customize your game bar settings. You can also customize or make changes to the default shortcuts. For example, the Windows key + G key is set by default for accessing the game bar. You can change this shortcut and other shortcuts within the game bar settings based on your preference.

The **capture** settings allow you to make important changes such as the audio quality, microphone and system volume, video quality, and the ability to record in the background while playing games.

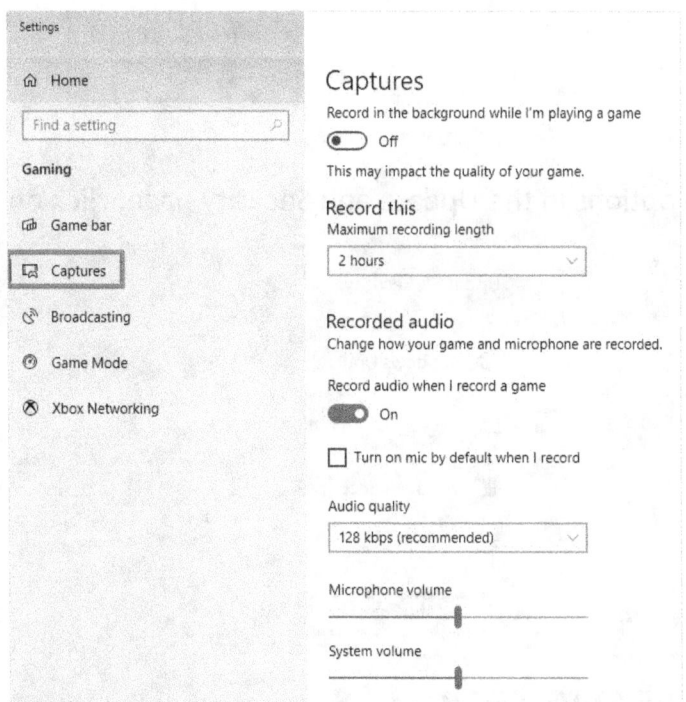

9.1.6 RUNNING THE TROUBLESHOOTER

A troubleshooter is a useful tool in windows 10 for fixing problems associated with different features of your device, such as windows update, Internet connections, Bluetooth, and more.

To access the Troubleshoot option;
1. Go to Start > Settings
2. Click on **Update & Security**.

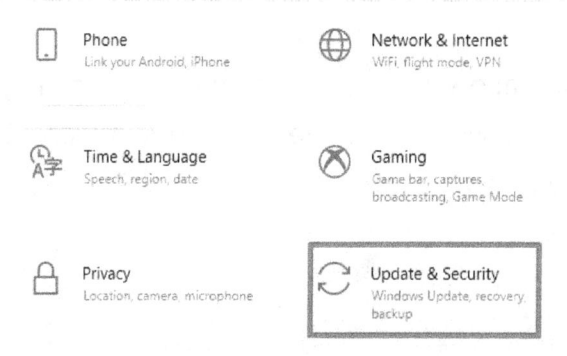

3. From the options in the Update and Security page, click on **Troubleshoot**.

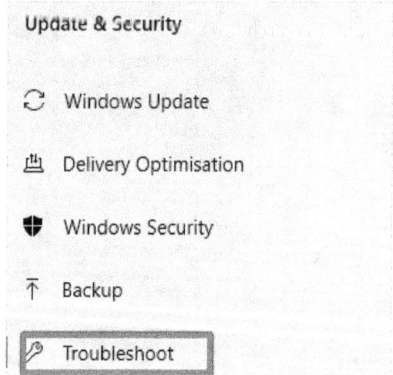

9.1.7 USING THE MAGNIFIER

Windows 10 has a cool feature that allows users to magnify the texts on their screens. People who find it difficult to read texts clearly may find this application very useful to help magnify the contents on their screens.

To use the Magnifier app;

Go to Start > Settings > Ease of Access > Magnifier

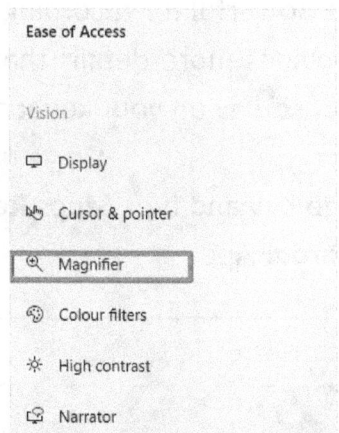

Alternatively, press the Windows Logo key Plus (+) key on your keyboard.

Use the (+) icon to magnify the contents of your screen. You can also use the view drop-down provided alongside the magnifier.

You can use different view options in the magnifier. These options are full screen, lens, and docked.

The lens option makes you read a particular section with a lens, allowing you to concentrate more on a particular area of your screen. You can move the lens around to magnify certain areas of your screen while keeping other text sizes constant.

Use the settings icon provided to customize your magnifier.

Use the Windows logo key + ESC to turn off the magnifier.

9.1.8 USING STEPS RECORDER

Windows Steps recorder is a powerful for recording or taking screenshots of your screen. The step recorder provides more details than what is available when you take screenshots using the **'prt sc'** key on your keyboard.

To access the step recorder;
1. Press the Windows Logo Key and type **Steps Recorder** in the search box.
2. Click on the **Steps Recorder** App.

3. Click on **Start Record** to start recording your screen.
4. To end the screen recording, click on the **Stop Record** button.

You can also add a comment using the **add comment** tools provided with the Steps Recorder.

The application should give a detailed analysis of the activities carried out. You can save the screen recordings using the save tool provided and also select the best screenshots for your work. The Steps Recorder app also provides additional details.

You can make some customizations from windows settings.
1. Go to **Steps Recorder settings** by clicking on the question icon in Steps Recorder.
2. Click on **Settings**

You can now personalize how your Steps Recorder works.

9.1.9 CUSTOMIZING YOUR STARTUP APPS

Windows startup apps are installed apps that are configured to start when your device is started.

To customize your startup apps;

Go to Start > Startup apps

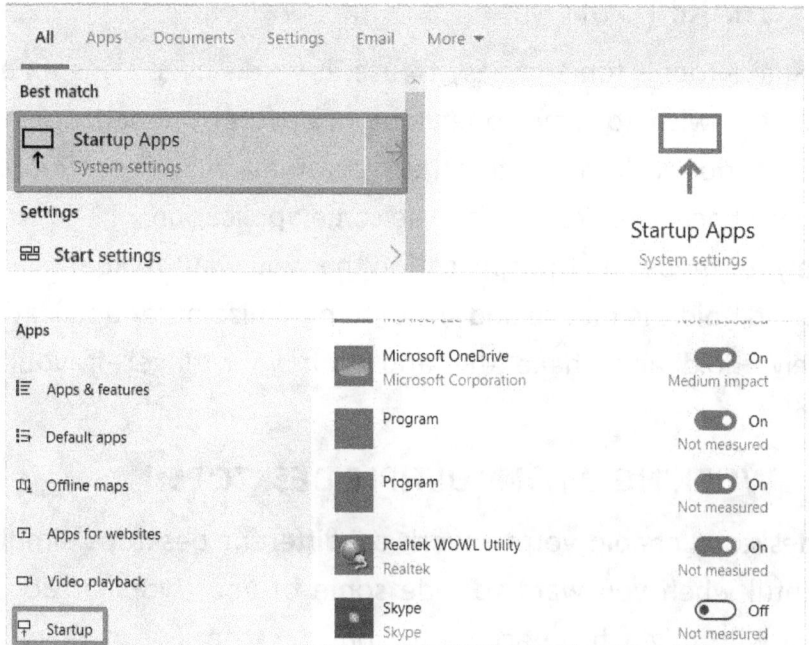

You can use the **Sort by** drop-down to sort how the startup apps are arranged.

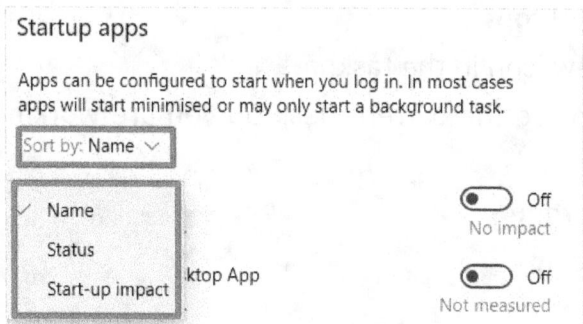

From the list, some applications are tagged high impact. These applications significantly increase the startup time, unlike the Low impact and medium impact.

You can toggle off any of the applications to prevent them from starting when you log in to your device, hence reducing the time it takes your computer to boot.

9.1.10 SHAKE TOOL:

Windows shake tool is fun and easy to use. It works by shaking an application or the window you wish to leave open out of several opened apps or windows. Shaking this window will minimize others automatically. Then, you can bring the minimized apps back on by re-shaking the same application.

1. Place your mouse on the application that you want to keep.
2. Click and hold the mouse and shake to minimize other applications.

Alternatively, hold and shake the app with your finger if your device is a touchscreen.

9.1.11 WORKING WITH MULTIPLE DESKTOPS:

Multiple desktops enable you to work on different desktops simultaneously. It may be helpful when you want to hide some of your work or documents from some people who might have access to your desktop. For instance, you may be using your laptop for executing office tasks that you want to hide from your children.

To use Multiple desktops;
Click on the Task view icon in the taskbar.

You will be able to see the current desktop you are working on and the opened applications.

To add a new desktop;
Click on **New desktop**

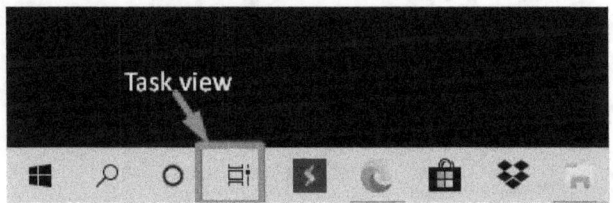

To remove any of the opened desktops on your computer, click the **Close button.**

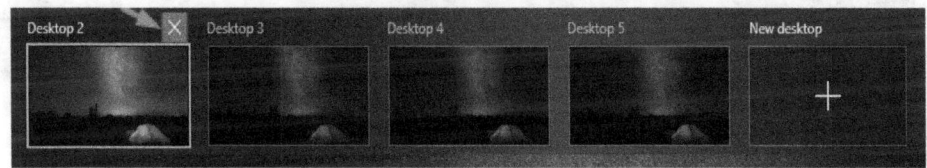

9.1.12 ACCESSING APPLICATIONS ON THE TASKBAR

As a user who has most of his frequently used applications pinned on the taskbar, you may want to quickly open or access the pinned applications without clicking on them. You can achieve this by using the shortcut keys. These keys will open the applications based on their relative positions on the taskbar.

To open any of your pinned applications;
Press Windows key + number representing its position on the taskbar.

For example, if I desire to open Microsoft edge quickly, the second application pinned on my taskbar, I will press the **Windows Logo key + 2.** You can as well apply this trick to open all the applications pinned to your taskbar.

9.1.13 USING WINDOWS 10 VOICE RECORDER

Windows 10 voice recorder is a useful application that does more than just recording. With this app, you can share and edit your recordings.

To use the voice recorder;
1. Go to Start > Voice recorder

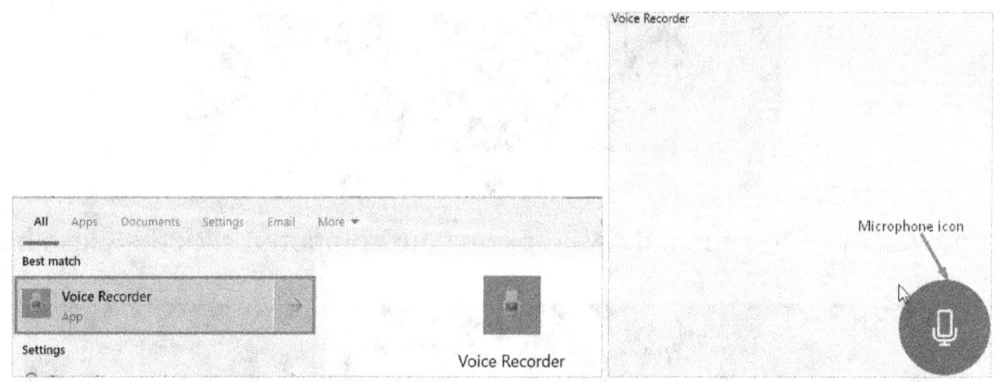

2. Click on the microphone to start recording.

If you are using the Windows 10 voice recorder application for the first time, you need to allow it to access your microphone. However, you can still remove this access from the microphone settings.

To access microphone settings;

1. Click the three dots in the lower right corner of the app.

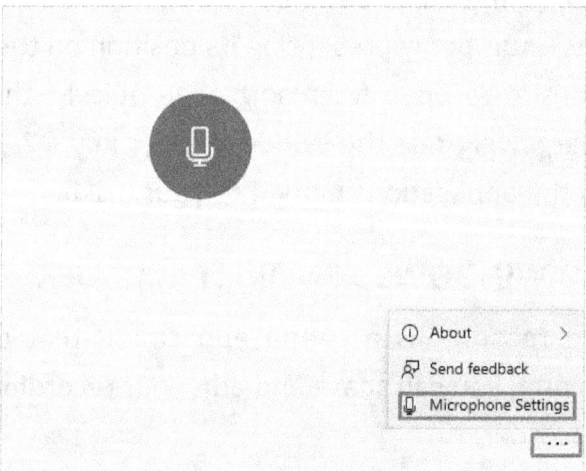

2. Click on **microphone settings** to customize the applications that can access your microphone.

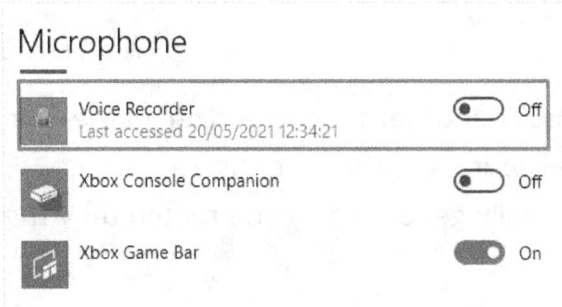

Use the icons provided to share, trim, rename or delete your audio files.

9.1.14   QUICK ASSIST

Windows Quick assist lets you assist or get assistance from another Windows 10 user. If you are offering help, you will take over the control of the other person's device. The same applies if you are getting assistance from another user. You must ensure the availability of an active internet connection to use quick assist.

To access Windows Quick assist;

Go to Start > Quick assist.

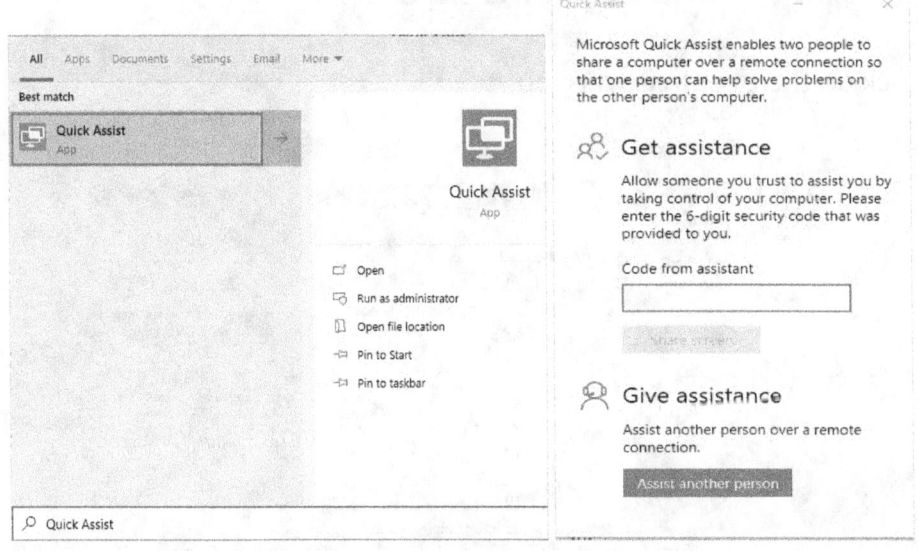

To give assistance;
1. Click on the '**Assist another person button'** in the Give assistance section.
2. Enter the email address of the other user.

The system automatically generates a code required by the second user to share his or her screen.

9.1.15   TROUBLESHOOTING OPTIONS FOR WINDOWS 10

Our device may likely run into some problems getting us worried and without us knowing the problem. There are some troubleshooting and techniques available within windows 10 to help you diagnose and generate reports of problems encountered by your device.

To troubleshoot;
1. Type **Event Viewer** in the search box

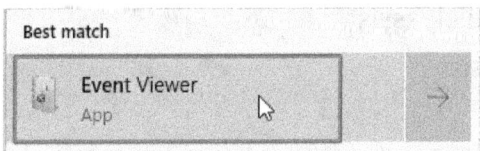

2. Click on the **event viewer** app.

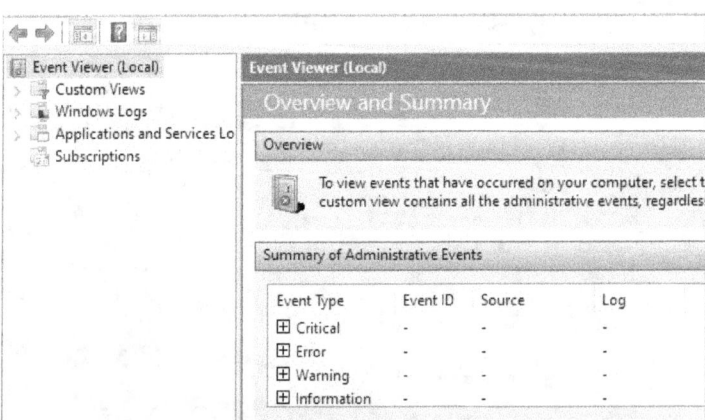

By default, Windows 10 keeps a log of all the activities and issues within your device. You can be more specific by clicking on the **Windows log** or the **Applications and services log**.

Read through the **overview and summary** to know the administrative events that have happened over time. You can also look at the log summary report generated to scan for possible issues.

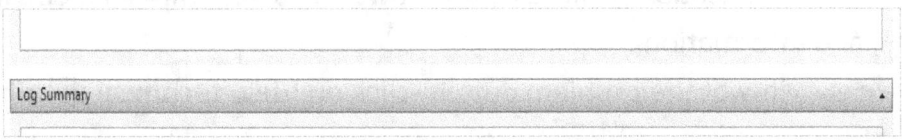

Another available option to diagnose an issue with your device is the **view reliability history** within the control panel. To access this page;

Go to Start > View reliability history.

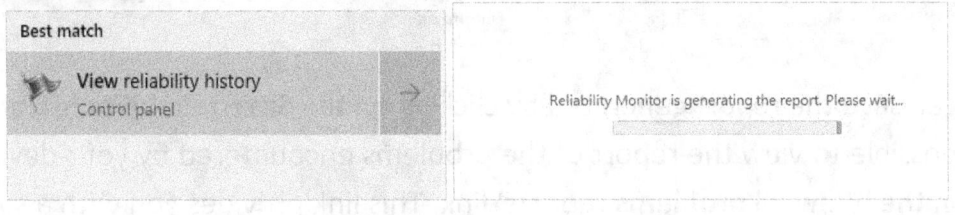

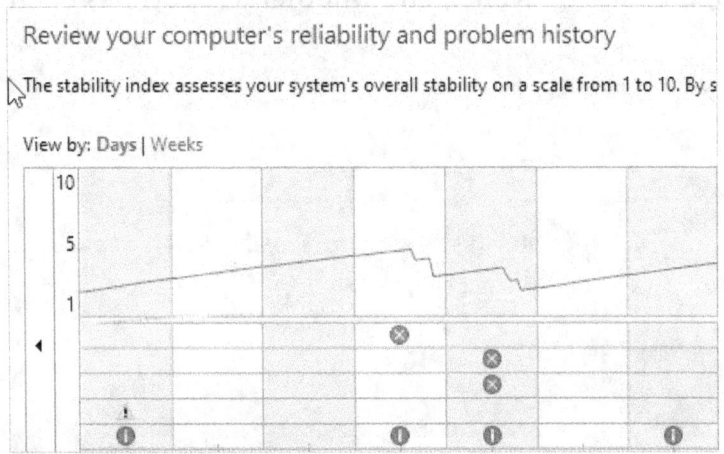

On the reliability monitor page, a plot is made to assess the reliability of your device and assigned a scalability index between 1 and 10. You can customize your view option either by days or weeks.

You can look for a problem or error within your device by clicking on the area within the plot. The reliability monitor takes note and keeps track of five major histories, i.e., Application failures, Windows failures, Miscellaneous failures, Warnings, and Information.

To get a clear view of the problem details, click on **View technical detail.**

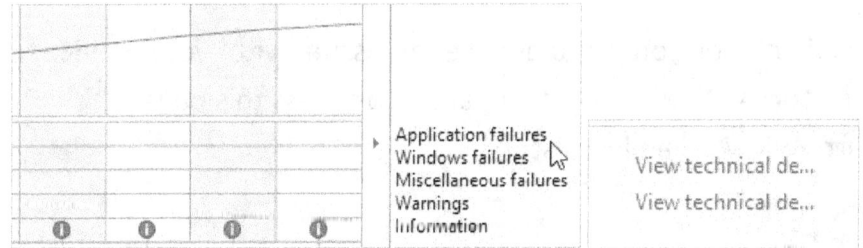

You can save the report generated by clicking on the **Save reliability history**.

It is possible to view the report of the problems encountered by your device. Just click on **the 'View all problems reports'** link. This link provides you with a summary of the problem, the date of events, and whether a report has been sent or not.

9.2 WINDOWS 10 SHORTCUTS

The table below shows some important shortcut keys available on windows 10.

SHORTCUT KEYS	FUNCTIONS
Ctrl + (A)	To select all items.
Ctrl + C	To copy all selected items.
Ctrl + (D)	To delete and move the selected item to recycle bin.
Shift + (D)	To permanently delete without moving to the recycle bin.
Ctrl + (N)	To open up a new window
Ctrl + (Z)	To undo an executed task
F2 or (fn + F2)	To rename
Ctrl + (V)	To paste already selected item or text
Alt + (D)	To select the address bar.
Ctrl + (N)	To open a new window.
Ctrl + (W)	To close an existing page or application.
Ctrl + (M)	Mark mode
Alt + (P)	To access the preview panel.

Windows Logo Key + (A)	To access the action center.
Windows key	To open or close the start menu.
Windows Logo key + C	To talk to Cortana
Windows logo key + (E)	To open your File Explorer.
Windows logo key + (H)	Dictation
Windows + (F)	Opening Windows feedback hub
Windows Logo key + (G)	Opening game bar
Window logo key + (I)	To access the settings page.
Windows logo key + (K)	Access the Connect quick action page
Windows logo key + (L)	Lock your device
Windows logo key + (M)	To minimize all opened windows.
Windows logo key + (P)	To choose the mode for projection.
Windows logo key + (R)	Accessing the Run dialogue box
Windows logo key + Ctrl +(Q)	To access Quick assist.
Windows logo key + (S)	To start searching
Windows logo + (U)	To access the ease of access page.

Windows logo key + (T)	To move through pinned applications on the taskbar.
Windows logo key + (X)	To access the quick link menu.
Windows logo key + (;)	To use emojis
Windows logo key + number	To open pinned applications on the taskbar based on their positions.
Windows logo key + Tab	To open the task view.
Windows logo key + left arrow key	To align an opened window to the left side of the screen
Windows logo key + Right arrow key	To align an opened window or app to the right side of the screen.
Ctrl + (R)	To refresh the active page.
Alt + Tab	Switching back and forth between opened applications
Alt + (F4)	To exit active the application.
Windows key + (D)	To show or hide the desktop screen.
Windows key + V	To access the clipboard.
Windows key + Pause or Windows logo key + fn + Pause	To access the system properties page.
Windows key + (home key)	To minimize all opened windows and applications except the active page or window.

Windows logo key + (+)	To use the magnifier.
Ctrl + (Esc)	To open the start menu.
Shift + (F10)	To show an item's shortcut.
Windows key + Ctrl + (D)	For adding a new virtual desktop
Windows key + Ctrl + (F4)	To close an active virtual desktop.
Windows key + Ctrl + Enter	To use the narrator
Prt Sc	To take a screenshot of the contents of your screen.
F10 or Shift + (F10)	To open or activate the menu bar in the active window.
F5	To refresh
Alt + (F8)	To make password visible while signing in.

www.ingramcontent.com/pod-product-compliance
Lightning Source LLC
Chambersburg PA
CBHW080546220526
45466CB00010B/3047